A WORD FROM THE AUTHOR

This is a personal story-my story - for as a child of Jamaican Christian parents who came to Britain in the 1950s, I personally saw and experienced many of the things I write about in this book. In the following chapters, I explain the reasons why my parents like many of their generation left the Caribbean for Britain. I describe the country they came to, explain how they lived, the religious atmosphere they found, the racism they faced, and I show how they coped.

ACKNOWLEDGEMENTS

This book could not have been written without the help, support and encouragement of several people who read the manuscript and made many useful suggestions. I would like to thank Chris Day, my publisher for igniting the initial spark, Dr Allister Hinds from the University of the West Indies, Mona, and Mrs Norma Messam of the University of Technology (UTECH) Jamaica, for providing the best environment I could ever wish for to write this book. I would also like to thank Marcia Dixon for the many stimulating discussions we've had on the various topics in this book and my sincere thanks go to Leanna Benjamin, Becky Wybrow for the design, Aditi Shah for the layout and to Zara and everyone at Filament Publishing. As would be expected, I have made every effort to be as accurate as I can, and therefore any omissions and errors, I acknowledge are entirely my own.

For: Jaeden, Cielo and Cecelia

Stay in touch! Sign up to Roy's newsletter at:
www.royfrancis.co.uk

WINDRUSH AND THE BLACK PENTECOSTAL CHURCH IN BRITAIN

Roy N Francis

Published by
Filament Publishing Ltd
16, Croydon Road, Beddington,
Croydon , Surrey, CR0 4PA
www.filamentpublishing.com
email: info@filamentpublishing.com
+44 (0) 20 8688 2598

Windrush and the Black Penticostal Church in Britain
by Roy Francis
ISBN 978-1-913623-26-5

Printed by 4edge Ltd

TABLE OF CONTENETS

INTRODUCTION

They were a mixed bunch who came, ordinary folks, students, pastors, teachers, church members, and former soldiers who had fought in the second world war and were now back in Britain. Work and the chance of a better life was the reason why my parents and others from the Caribbean came to Britain and work was the prime motivation. Most were Christians at least nominally, and many were members of the established church in the West Indies. I tell their story and explain what happened to them when they went to church in Britain for the first time. I contrast this with what their fellow Pentecostals did and show how they had a unique way of keeping their religious flame burning.

Much of what I write about in this book is the result of what happened after I wrote, 'How to make gospel music work for you,' which was written for gospel artists trying to make a success of their music in today's digital and social media age. To do this, I decided to show the historical link between Caribbean Christianity and the music Caribbean people came to Britain with, as both are inextricably linked. Today the music we now know as British gospel, has its origins in this synthesis. When the book was released, this assessment attracted a great deal of attention and the book you now have in your hand is a fuller understanding of this, the historical context of Caribbean Christian migration to Britain.

Windrush and the Black Pentecostal Church in Britain is a series of tales, recollections, and personal anecdotes in which I tell the story of the early Caribbean Christians who came to Britain in the 1950s and 60s. I give a glimpse of what life was like for them and in telling this story I draw on many years of experience as a first-generation Windrush child. Much of what I write about I personally saw including the difficulties many West Indians faced in finding somewhere to live, the difficulties of settling in, the weather, loneliness, keeping the faith and how as Christians they started their churches. I also explain the music they came with and show how it was used in their worship, how it was a sustaining force and what happened to it when it came into contact with the songs of the Billy Graham Crusades, the music of Jim Reeves, Tennessee Ernie Ford, and later on, the effect that Edwin Hawkins and 'Oh Happy Day' had on it.

In the following pages, I also tell what it was like for children like me growing up in Britain. I share some of my experiences, first as a nine-year-old, who my father would regularly take to play in churches and open-air services, and how as a little Black boy playing the accordion and the piano, I attracted quite a bit of attention. I also explain what it was like as a first-generation Black boy in a British secondary school and show how this experience has influenced my life ever since.

As part of the story of Caribbean Christians, I also explain another migration which took place in the 1980s with African Christians coming to Britain. Like Caribbean before, African Christians could not believe how unchristian Britain was when they arrived and soon set about establishing their churches. Today Africans are most of the Black population in Britain, they have a high incidence of church attendance and now have some of the largest and fastest-growing churches in the country. London is the place where this is best seen and where there has been the greatest growth. I tell this story and show how African settlement mirrors that of the Caribbean and show some of the key features that have made African churches successful. I also suggest, like Caribbean before some of the likely challenges, they'll face in the future and assess their chances of success.

For clarification, I frequently use the term 'West Indies' or 'West Indian' in this book rather than 'Caribbean' which is the more correct term. I do this to distinguish mainly between people of the former British colonies in the Caribbean and those whose colonial experiences were with other European powers. I also use the term 'gospel music' ostensibly to refer to Black gospel, as this is generally known and understood in the music business. I know the term today is elastic, but I use it as how musicologists understand it, as a separate and distinct genre of music with its roots embedded in the 'Spirituals,' from where it has grown and developed.

Finally, I believe Windrush and the Black Pentecostal Church in Britain, is a timely story and one which turns the spotlight on an area of British life not often written about but one which is a great success story, -Caribbean and African migration to Britain-, and the on-going spiritual restoration of a once-great Christin country.

Roy Francis
2020-Kingston Jamaica

'London is the Place for Me'

London is the place for me
London this lovely city
You can go to France or America,
India, Asia or Australia
But you must come back to London city
Well believe me I am speaking broadmindedly
I am glad to know my Mother Country
I have been travelling to countries years ago
But this is the place I wanted to know
London that is the place for me-[1]

On the 21st of June 1948, *The Empire Windrush* an old second world war Troop Carrier, slipped quietly almost unnoticed into Tilbury Docks in the East End of London. This was once the principal port for handling goods and grain coming into the country, but onboard this day was a special consignment of 1000 passengers who had paid £28, (£1000 at today's prices), to get into Britain. On its way up the English Channel, the government was nervous at the thought of the approaching ship. There was already unrest in parliament as 11 Labour MPs had written to the Prime Minister protesting about the arrival, and unable to predict how the country would react, the government sent a warship to escort *Windrush* into port, and insisted it remained there until it decided what to do. [2]

The next day, the 22nd of June, the passengers were allowed to disembark, and as they made their way down the gangway and into the flurry of bustling London, Aldwyn Roberts, the calypso singer Lord Kitchener, burst into song: *'London, is the Place for Me'*, the song he had composed for his arrival in Britain much to the delight of the waiting reporters, and the Pathe News crew, who had gone to Tilbury to cover the story. Although the figure of those arriving was listed as 492, the official passenger list was 1027 of which 802 listed their country of residence as the West Indies. They included, 539 Jamaicans, 139 Bermudans, 73 Trinidadians, 44 from British Guiana, and the rest from Mexico, South America, and the other West Indian Islands. Among these were, 684 males, 257 females, 50 boys and 36 girls. [3]

They were a mixed bunch who came, ordinary folks, students, pastors, teachers, church members, and former soldiers who had fought in the second world war and were now on their way back to Britain. As West Indians they came because there were plenty of jobs, and they knew what working would mean to them and their families and how this could change their lives. They also came to fill the thousands of jobs on the railways, in the hospitals, on the busses, in factories, and those who wanted an education, came also, because that too was on offer.

As West Indians, they were passionately committed to the country and saw it as their patriotic duty, to go and 'help rebuild the 'motherland,' or at least that's what the posters said back home. As West Indians, they loved the queen, held the country in great affection, spoke the same language, observed all the national holidays, had the same religion and their institutions were based on British ones. Even their middle classes took tea in the afternoon like the British, and what's more, what they were doing in Britain, wasn't anything strange, for they were in the 'mother country', and saw nothing unusual about that.

Once on British soil, nothing could have prepared the West Indians for what they were about to experience, nor could they have known what to expect. One of the first things they noticed, was how grey everything looked, and how dull everything seemed. The day was cold with very little sunlight, and the rows of smoke they saw belching out of chimney tops, were homes where people lived, and not factories where they worked as they had thought. However, as mainly young men, they were glad to be in Britain, and thrilled at the thought of finding work, and they couldn't wait to get started.

Many of those who came were ill-prepared for Britain and had no idea of what they were letting themselves in for. What they knew about the country was what they had either learnt in school, picked up here and there, or heard on the radio, much of which were often imaginary and idyllic. Now here they were in a country exhausted by war and in need of repair. The Second world war had ended three years earlier but you only had to look at the the burnt-out buildings, the homes, shops, factories, and the physical landscape of the country, to see what the war had done. The obvious sign was the number of bombsites still scattered around London which bore the full brunt of the Luftwaffe bombings, but nobody had told them about this, nor how living in such a strange environment would affect their stay in Britain. Yet they came prepared to work and to do their bit for the country, and overall, they were generally optimistic.

Not every West Indian came the way of Empire Windrush or were their route to the country straightforward. Many came, via Genoa in Italy, and from there took the train to France via

Switzerland, and from there the ferry to Dover, ending up at Waterloo station in London. Others sailed directly from the West Indies and came ashore at Southampton, and from there took the train to central London. Others still, came by plane when the air traffic between the West Indies and London increased, which is how my brother and I came to meet our parents, who had arrived in London in 1953.

I don't remember much about the journey coming to Britain although my younger brother says he remembers everything. I can't even remember the trip from our tiny village in Smithville Clarendon to Kingston the capital of Jamaica, nor do I remember the plane ride or how we reached our parent's home in North London. What I do remember, and this has stayed with me for years, is the bar of chocolate my father brought me on the first day, from George who owned the little kiosk at the top of our street. The other thing I remember and which is the story of many West Indian children, is that once in Britain, my brother and I had to learn to build a new relationship with our parents, to replace the one we already had with our grandparents, who we thought were our parents!

Life was hard when the West Indians arrived and most people had little money and what little they had, they spent locally on food and household goods near to where they lived. Food was short and so were goods and materials, and although everyone tried to cope as best, they could, they were exhausted at the repeated stoppages of gas, water, and electricity. Everyone had a ration book which the government had introduced during the war, and though things were changing, this was still the way many people got their basic foods such as sugar, cheese, bacon and meat, by exchanging their ration coupons for their weekly supplies.

Housing too was in short supply as the war had destroyed 25% of the housing stock leaving many people homeless, or they were forced to live in the overcrowded slums that grew up around the cities. Labour was in power when the West Indians arrived, surprisingly defeating Churchill the war hero in the 1945 General Election. It seemed as if the country wanted a complete break from the past and Labour responded to this with a radical programme of reconstruction and development. It quickly got to work implementing the changes it had promised the country.

Labour's first task was to clear the slums. The second to build homes, and with an estimated three-quarter of a million homes needed, rolled out a massive house building programme despite a shortage of labour and raw materials. The house building programme centred on first building 'Prefabs' or prefabricated homes. These were temporary dwellings constructed in factories and assembled on site. They were cheap to build, cheap to rent, came with an inside toilet and refrigerator, and were largely made available to the poor. They quickly became popular and complemented the government's own house-building programme which was enshrined in the 1946 New Town Act. The aim of the act was to move people out of the slums and house them in the new towns Labour was building in Bracknell in Berkshire, Harlow in Essex, Milton Keynes in Buckinghamshire, Telford in Shropshire, and Cwmbran in Wales. Over one million homes were built this way, and this helped to initially alleviate the acute housing shortage.

With the slum clearance and house building programme underway, Labour next turned its attention to the economy. It reformed the education system, set up a National Health

Service and rolled out its Nationalisation programme. This programme aim was to bring all the major industries, coal, steel, iron, gas, railways, electricity etc, under the control of the state, with the aim of creating jobs, rebuilding the economy, lifting the country out of poverty, and setting it on its way into the modern age.

Within three years Nationalisation was bearing fruits and was a success. Output rose, export increased, unemployment fell, consumer goods rose also, especially among labour-saving devices like washing machines and vacuum cleaners. There were also corresponding increases in cars, radios and television production, and the construction industry saw a similar increase, with hundreds of new offices built to provide work for the army of female workers coming on to the job market for the first time. Over two million people were employed by the state, and the economy continued to grow and recover.

In the next general election (1951), Labour was surprisingly defeated, and the country returned the Conservatives to power. They largely continued with Labour's economic policies as well as introducing a range of economic and social reforms of their own. The economy continued to grow bringing real benefits to many people, and for the first time since the war, workers saw an increase in their wages and a corresponding rise in their standard of living. A real sense of economic well-being gripped the country and many people felt they were on the road to a brighter future. It soon became clear though, that despite this economic success, there were severe shortages, including workers available to meet the demands of the economy, and the output being produced.

The government's answer was to turn to its former colonies in the West Indies to try and solve this problem. What it did was to introduce *'The British Nationality Act'*- which conferred citizenship -and therefore unrestricted right of entry-to anyone from the West Indies and the Commonwealth, who was prepared to travel to Britain to work.

Chapter 56 of the Act states:

"Every person who under this Act is a citizen of the United Kingdom and Colonies...shall by virtue of that citizenship have the status of a British subject."

I suppose somewhere deep in the government's unconscious mind was the idea that historically during slavery, the West Indies produced the best workers, and as such, attracting West Indians once again to work for Britain, might just solve the labour problem. At first, the take up was slow, but as word got round in the West Indies that jobs were plentiful and available in Britain, things soon began to change. The 802 West Indians who arrived at Tilbury in 1948, the bulk of which were Jamaicans, were the first to take advantage of this, and it is against this background that the majority of West Indians came to Britain in the 1960s, many of whom like my parents, were Christians.

When the West Indians first arrived, Britain was already used to large numbers of people coming into the country. After the second world war, Irish, Poles and Jewish refugees from Nazi Germany came to settle in Britain. The only difference this time was that the new migrants were Black, and although their numbers at first were small, this changed as the demand for workers increased, as Britain relentlessly pursued its post-war redevelopment programme.

From 1948 when the Empire Windrush arrived until 1952, between 1,000 and 2,000 people entered Britain each year, followed by a steady and rapid rise until 1957, when 42,000 migrants from the New Commonwealth, mainly from the Caribbean came. The numbers declined by almost a half in the two succeeding years but by 1960 it had increased again to 58,000. By 1973 over 600,000 people had migrated to Britain.[4]

Most West Indians who came were mainly agricultural workers who farmed smallholdings in their own countries. Others were domestic and office workers, carpenters, dressmakers, shoemakers, and tailors. The majority however were Jamaicans and many of these had never even visited Kingston the capital of their own country, and yet they were prepared to risk travelling all the way to the other side of the world in search of work. Others who were West Indians, left their homeland for Britain also, but the bulk of Jamaicans came because of two reasons, the *McCarran-Walter Act (1952)*, which prevented them going to America to work, and 1948 Nationality Act, which acted as a spur to Britain.

When the West Indians first arrived in 1948, they were merely following in the footstep of their predecessors who as far back as in Roman times were in Britain. Peter Fryer in his excellent and scholarly book, 'Staying Power'-The History of Black people in Britain, states:

'There were Africans in Britain before the English!

Fryer goes on to show that Africans were in Britain long before many people realised and that they were there during the Roman times. They were also in Scotland in 1505, and in England during the reign of Henry VII, Henry VIII and Elizabeth I. In 1578, for example, George Best, a diarist, wrote of meeting *'an Ethiopian as blacke as a cole brought into England,'* and in the sixteen century, there were supposedly so many Blacks in England that, Queen Elizabeth in 1596 wrote to her mayors issuing them 'with licences to expel' Blacks out of the country. [5]

In the sixteenth, seventeenth and eighteen centuries also, Blacks were brought into England by plantation owners to work as household slaves, cooks, maids and pages. Although there were those who occasionally gained their freedom, like Ignatius Sancho, a protégé of the Duke and Duchess of Montagu, and Olaudah Equiano, a slave to a British naval officer, the rest lived all their lives as slaves in Britain, and therefore the property of their owners. In the eighteenth century also, there was a sizable Black presence in the City of London, so much so that, *'The Gentleman's Magazine'* reported that there were *'supposed to be near 20,000... 'Negroe servants in London.'*

Much nearer our time and during the first world war, many Black people fought for 'King and Country,' and in 1915 the British West Indies Regiment was formed as a separate unit to fight alongside the British Army. It saw active service in East Africa, the Middle East and on the Western Front.

Following the outbreak of hostilities in 1914, many West Indians left the colonies to enlist in the army in the UK and were recruited into British regiments. In October and November 1915 many of the contingents were brought together at Seaford, West Sussex, and were formed into the British West Indies Regiment (BWIR). The regiment's battalions saw service in East Africa, Egypt, Palestine, Jordan, France and Italy..... A total of 397 officers and 15,204 other ranks served in the BWIR.- [6]

In the second World War, Black people again fought for King and Country. They served as air servicemen, soldiers, and munitions workers, with over 500,000 coming from the British Empire and Dominions, including 10,000 from the West Indies, and many more who came to serve in the Merchant Navy.

During the second world war, more than 10,000 West Indians volunteered to leave home and join the fight against Hitler, with thousands more serving as merchant seamen. The RAF gained more recruits from the Caribbean than any other part of the British Empire, with around 400 flying as aircrew and 6,000 working as ground staff. [7]

In the 1960s when the bulk of West Indians came to Britain, those who had nowhere to live was sent by the government to Clapham South, and there below the underground station, were given food and shelter. It didn't take long for those in London to find work as this was plentiful, and as the 'Labour Exchange' *(jobcentre)* was only a short distance away in Brixton, they could arrive there in the morning and be in work by lunchtime! Those who had an address or had relatives or friends elsewhere in Britain, headed there, mainly to the Midlands and the industrial North, and there they found work in factories, iron foundries, in textile mills, on the railways and in the agricultural industry. Few, however, went to Scotland, Wales or Northern Ireland.

Although obtaining work was relatively easy for West Indians, finding accommodation was difficult. Today, there are many stories within the Caribbean Community, recalling the horrible experiences many people faced when they first arrived and went looking for somewhere to live. Often, they were met with insulting and humiliating signs which white landlords pinned to their windows, making it clear that they didn't want any, 'coloureds, blacks, dogs or Irish, and that, 'niggers need not apply'. And if this wasn't bad enough, when West Indians did manage to find somewhere to live, they were usually shabby places, with no bath, an outside toilet, and were often located in the worst part of the city, where for the first time, they found themselves living next to white people, with all the implications, this would have for the future.

Many West Indians shared the rooms they rented, and those working at nights would sleep in the day, while the nights were reserved for those who worked daily. Families, on the other hand, could only afford one room, and the one-room became the bedroom, the kitchen, dining room, and playroom for the children. Many people cooked in their rooms on small stoves, and if they weren't cooking in their rooms, they did so on the landing for that's where the kitchen, if the house had one was located. Most houses didn't have a bathroom either and if anyone wanted to bathe, they'd do so in a large long pan in their rooms. There were always the local 'public baths,' and for a small fee a person could hire a cubicle, and along with a bar of soap and a towel, have a bath. When they finished, a man would come round with a large wooden brush, scrub clean the tub, and run the water for the next occupant!

West Indians knew next to nothing about white people when they first came to Britain, and what little they knew was limited to the white people they saw in the West Indies usually those in an official capacity, or those who were rich or well-to-do. What they didn't know was the extent to which 'being black' had such a negative effect on British people. For example, this was the first time most whites -mainly working class-were seeing blacks, and to them this was strange, often stirring up all the historical negative stereotypes they had internalised about Black people. To many white people, black meant everything bad. Being blacklisted was negative, Black was evil, and black was the devil! It didn't take a great leap of the imagination for them to link these stereotypical images, to what they were seeing before their eyes!

West Indians themselves were not immune to the impact of stereotypical images they too had inculcated. For example, generally white is associated with that which is good, pure, clean, and beautiful. Consequently, many West Indians had an exaggerated view of white people and thought that in Britain, all white people lived well, were well to do, and that their 'streets were paved with gold.' They soon got a nasty shock when they arrived and saw how white people lived, in many cases much worse than they. On the other hand, although the West Indies was part of the British Empire, most British people knew next to nothing of the West Indies, their history, nor the link between the Islands and Britain. They knew nothing about the historical role that sugar, and the plantation system played in making Britain rich. Nor for that matter that during the 18th and 19th century, sugar was one of the driving force of Britain's industrial success, with the plantations in the West Indies producing 80–90 per cent of the sugar consumed in Britain and in Western Europe. Sugar was as important then to the British economy, as oil is to it today, and it was sugar that made British Plantation owners rich, with the term, 'as rich as a West Indian,' an indication of how wealthy a person was. London, Liverpool and Bristol became rich from the proceeds of sugar and the slave trade that accompanied it.

Between 1700 and 1709 the trade in sugar increased dramatically due to the increasing popularity of sugar to sweeten luxury drinks such as tea and coffee. In 1700, Britain's sugar consumption was 4 pounds (weight) per person, a century later that had risen to 18 pounds per person. The increased availability and popularity of sugar was due to a gradual increase in the standard of living whereas before only the very rich could afford such luxuries....... [8]

In 1833 slavery was abolished and the British government, compensated plantation owners handsomely 'for the loss of their property.' In 2019, David Lammy a Black MP, speaking in the British Parliament, made the point that the compensation paid to Plantation owners was worth £17 billion in today's money, but what did the slaves get in return, nothing!

Not everyone welcomed the West Indians when they first arrived in Britain, and as their numbers grew in the 1960s, the level of racism they faced was extremely high. Although most had never met a Black person before, a lot of this hatred was at first merely blind prejudice and competition for the limited supply of accommodation, but as the years went by, this hatred grew into rejection and outright loathing. The situation got so bad, that it seemed as if Britain was operating an unofficial 'colour bar.' There were race riots in Liverpool, Nottingham, and in London Far-right racist groups like the 'White Defence League' and the 'Union Movement' helped to stoke up anti-immigration feelings which spilt over into a full-scale race riot on the streets of Notting Hill Gate in 1958. The Notting Hill Carnival which today is such a huge success, was started by Claudia Jones the editor of the West Indian Gazette, as a response to the riot, and as a way of fostering good relations between the races in the area, and look what it has become today!

My own experience of racism during the early years in Britain centred on my secondary schooling, for this is when I became conscious of its insidious and ever-present overt and subtle manifestations. Here I was in the 1960s part of the first wave of West Indians children to go to Secondary school in Britain. My school was all boys with over a thousand pupils. It was based on the old public-school ethos of learning, sportsmanship and duty. Most of the 'Masters' were ex military men. They wore academic gowns in lessons and carried this military culture into everyday school life. I was one of only a handful of Black boys and playtimes I largely spent on my own as the white boys seemed largely afraid of me. Not fearing me but fearing the 'unknown' in me. A couple of boys were curious enough to venture, but this was more out of curiosity, rather than seeking to make friends. However, one thing about racism is that, if you are exposed to it long enough and constantly on the receiving end you quickly develop strategies on how to deal with it, and what becomes your survival. In my case, I quickly realised that a bag of sweets not only did the trick but bought me friends!!!

The same is no less true of my teachers who generally viewed me consciously and subconsciously with all the racist assumptions they had about Black people. In my case, many times they made direct racists remarks aimed at me in front of the class, and in and out of lessons without batting an eyelid or giving a thought how I felt. No teacher today would last a day in any school in Britain if they were to utter anything like what some of what my teachers regularly and unashamedly said to me. It's no point repeating any of them here, as so much has changed in this regard, and the battle is now elsewhere, not so much in overt racism but in the subtle, institutional, and unintentional manifestations of it. However, despite all this, the school left an indelible impression on me and influenced my future prospect. It ignited a love of learning, and a love of hymns which were regularly sung at Morning and Special Assemblies.

The School also stirred up in me a love of classical music, and I remember spending many compulsory lessons listening to music I'd never heard before or had any idea about. Most of it washed over me and I found the lessons at times bewildering. One piece of music however stood out, - Schubert Quintet, - 'The Trout.' This was music with a tune, music I could follow, and as I played the piano albeit, by air, the brilliance of the music and the playing, captured my imagination. I trace my abiding love of classical music today from this exposure.

Apart from the *British Nationality Act* which the government used to attract West Indians to work in Britain, it also sent out officials to the region to encourage more and more people to come, as the economy was demanding more and more skilled and unskilled labour. Both London Transport, the Hotel industry, and the National Health Service, actively recruited in the West Indies. London Transport enlisted mainly in Barbados, paying Bajans fares to Britain and recovering it from their wages. Enoch Powell was a British official active in this process, especially in recruiting nurses from Barbados. This is the same Enoch Powell who in 1968, as Tory Shadow

Minister, made his infamous *'Rivers of Blood'* speech in which he warned the Government that if it didn't change its immigration policy, there would be 'blood on the streets of England'. To his credit, Edward Heath the Tory Leader sacked Powell for stirring up anti-immigration feelings and threw him out of the Shadow Cabinet. But the damage was done, Powell had given an official voice to the level of racism that began when the West Indians first arrived, and which by 1968 had grown into a crescendo and outright hostility.

Part of the problem was that white people had an extremely low opinion of West Indians and generally disapproved of them coming into the country. They were often hostile to them, saw West Indians as 'uncivilised, thought they ate strange foods, didn't want to have any contact with them,' didn't want to work with them either, and would never let them into their homes. However, as the 1960s progressed, and as more and more West Indians began to arrive to fill the thousands of unskilled jobs many white people didn't want to or refused to do, the more white people wanted an end to immigration. What they demanded was a change to the government's policy. The government responded by announcing that it would stop recruiting from the West Indies and would take steps to tighten immigration control. In other words, just as it had used the law to attract West Indians to Britain in the first place, it would again use the law to restrict their inflow.

In 1962, the government published its plan. Under the plan, the right of automatic entry to Britain from the West Indies and the Commonwealth was restricted, and a voucher scheme put in its place. The aim of the scheme was to limit the right of entry only to skilled migrants, such as doctors, lawyers, engineers, teachers etc. When West Indians realised the implications of this new policy, and what it would mean to the families they'd left behind in the West Indies, they quickly arranged to get them into the country. When the act came into force, West Indians worst fears were realised, for what they found was that, when they made applications to come to Britain, their education and qualifications were not recognised, or in many cases, deemed inadequate, and as a consequence, refused entry. What this showed was the government's real intention, which was to stop the inflow of migrants from the West Indian and Commonwealth, which it has continued to do to this day.

Life was hard for West Indians when they first arrived, and they faced a constant struggle to adapt to their new way of life. Here they were in a complex metropolitan society, and the daily grind of negotiating their way in it often frustrated them. Many were ordinary folks from the rural areas and unused to being without their families, and here they were in Britain largely on their own. The frequent smog in the winter months merely added to their problem, especially the 1952 one which killed over 4000 people.[9] Also, the terrible winters of the 1960s didn't help either, especially the 1962/63 one, when snow on the ground was up to 6 metres deep, roads and railways blocked, villages cut off, telephone lines brought down and rivers froze, including the river Thames. Most West Indians had never seen anything like this before, and they yearned for home, their families, and the warmth of the Caribbean sun. Their only consolation was that they were in work and earning enough money to send home to support their families, and with this, they braced themselves, and with renewed hope and determination, pressed forward.

Dealing with racial prejudice was something new to West Indians, and the racism that surrounds it. Racism is the idea that a person's racial characteristics determines their place in society, and with it, their life chances. It's a power relationship and West Indians were not prepared for this. Naively they thought that the same way they respected white people and treated them in their homeland, they would be accorded the same in Britain. When this didn't happen, and it often didn't, they were surprised, and this quickly turned to disillusionment as they looked for ways to cope. Their idea was to stay in Britain for only five years, save enough money, return home and with the money saved, perhaps even start a small business. Because of this, they kept their 'grips' (suitcases) packed as a sign of their eventual return, but towards the end of the 1960s, they began to have a change of heart.

What prompted this change was the realisation that despite the hardship and racism they were facing, paradoxically, they were now much better off than when they first arrived. They were in work and making money. They could afford to buy cars and fine clothes, and thanks to the *'pardner,'* were able to afford the deposit on a house, and with this, able to move to better areas in which to bring up their children. With this, any thought of 'going home,' was put on hold, if not for themselves, at least for their children's sake.

The 'Pardner,' (Esusu), which was so essential to the change in West Indians fortune and financial success in Britain, is a traditional form of financial cooperation found in many African societies for the benefit of each member. The practice was brought to the West Indies by slaves in the 17th century, and in Jamaica over time, became known as *pardner* and in other islands, syndicate or susu. West Indians brought this practice to Britain, and in the 1950s and 60s, it flourished in West Indian communities, mainly on account of the discriminatory practices of excluding West Indians from the banking and financial system. *Pardner*, assisted many West Indians to buy their homes, it paid the travel and other costs of family members joining them, and in later years, helped to buy their churches.

How a *pardner* work is that a group of people agrees to form a *pardner* and pay a sum of money ('hand') each week or month to someone trusted to be the 'banker.' Then it was weekly because that's how people were paid, whereas now it's largely monthly. With the banker chosen, each week, one of the members receives the total amount (or 'draw') which each of the members has contributed to the *pardner*. For example, if 12 people are in a *pardner* and save £50 a week over 20 weeks, each will receive £1000, which is a £1000 loan or looked at another way a £1000 savings. The banker decides on when each member is given a 'draw,' and when each member gets their 'draw,' it's customary for them to give the banker a donation for running the *pardner*, but this is not compulsory.

Apart from finding work and the *pardner* creating the financial base for West Indian success in Britain, not everyone experienced the benefits of migration and the economic advantage of being in the country. Those children for example who were part of a family but were left behind in the West Indies, -for not all came- paid a huge emotional price. Those small children who were left with relatives and grandparents, grew up thinking they were their parents, and when they got to Britain, they had to form new relationships with their 'real parents,' and this was not always successful, especially those children who came after their formative years. The situation was further complicated when West Indians began to have children in Britain. The result in many cases, were two sets of children from two cultural backgrounds, often unleashing a set of emotional and psychological problems, which many Caribbean have carried for years, and are only now, in their advancing years, willing to talk about.

Also, there were others who lost their way, and unable to cope ended up in mental institutions. Others still fell victim to a system they thought would liberate them, only to find that it failed them too. West Indian Christians were not immune to any of these, and it is against this background that they too came to Britain.

THEY CAME WITH THEIR CHRISTIANITY AND THEIR MUSIC

In the early years, West Indians who came to Britain as Christians, can be divided into two groups. Those who belonged to the established church in the West Indies, *(Anglicans, Methodists, Baptists, Catholics etc)*, and those who were Pentecostals, part of the network of independent churches in the West Indies. Not for one moment did either of these two groups think they'd be a problem with being a Christian in Britain or have any difficulties practising their faith. After all, they were in the 'mother country, the home of Christianity,' and why should there be a problem?

Christianity has a long history in the West Indies and is bound up with the capture and subjugation of the people of these Islands. The Spaniards and the French were the first to arrive, and when they conquered the West Indies, they came with Roman Catholicism. In 1665 the British arrived in Jamaica, they introduced *Anglicanism*, drove out the Spaniards who fled to the adjoining islands, and their slaves fled to the mountains. There in the mountains, the slaves formed an independent group known as the *'Maroons,'* and fought the English until the treaty of 1739 gave them a measure of autonomy, which their descendants hold to this day.

Once in the West Indies, the English turned it into a massive sugar plantation colony, making the settler class rich. It is estimated that from 1761 to 1807, traders based in British ports, transported over a million and a half African slaves across the Atlantic to work on the plantations in the West Indies, and pocketed over £60 million, about £8 billion in today's money.[10]

At first, Britain sent out clergies to the West Indies, not so much to convert slaves as there was an assumption that once slaves were baptised, they were deemed free, but to act as chaplains to the white plantation settler class. However, after the abolition of slavery in 1833, non-conformist missionaries arrived with the task of converting native West Indians to Christianity. The Baptists came next in the 1890s, as did The Seventh Day Adventist, and they were followed in the early 20th century by the Salvation Army and the Jehovah's Witness. In the 1940s, Pentecostalism arrived in Jamaica, brought there by American missionaries as part of the American revival experience.

In his book, *'West Indian and the Migrant Churches,'* Clifford Hill, an Anglican priest and sociologist, found that in the 1960s when West Indians arrived in Britain, over 69% of them, belonged to one of the six major religions, with the majority being either, Anglicans, Baptists or Methodists. Those who were Pentecostals, belonged to one of four churches, *The New Testament Church of God, The Church of God of Prophecy, The Apostolic Church, and Seventh Day Adventists,* although the latter is not strictly Pentecostal.

What these group of Christians found when they arrived, was a country that was still largely Christian and where Sunday was Victorian in character, given over to church, lunch, and quiet family relaxation. Shops were closed on Sundays and large sporting and music events were banned. But Britain was also a country where religion was in decline and one that was going through a period of profound, social, and economic change. It was also a time when young people were challenging the established order, with 'Freedom' their refrain, and they expressed this in their music, politics, and in their relaxed attitude to sex and sexual behaviour. Both the pill, the mini and the miniskirt, were totem symbols of this new-found freedom.

This social change, so visible in the 1960s, really began a decade earlier with the release of the film, 'Rock around the clock' starring Bill Haley. When the film hit British cinemas in 1956, it caused mini riots across the country with a celebrated one at the Gourmont Cinema in Lewisham. What the reaction to the film showed, was that the post-war redevelopment and economic boom had created a distinct social group the 'teenager.' These were young people in work, earning wages, had music and films aimed at them, and with very little social responsibilities, the teenager phenomenon was born and with it the rebellion that characterised it. This exploded in the 1960s, into 'the swinging sixties,' which was a time of student unrest, increase use of recreational drugs, the dominance of pop music, and was all summed up in the words of the Beatles song, 'all you need is love.'

West Indians were shocked at what they saw in the 1960s, for here they were, a group of God-fearing people bought up on a strict diet of Victorian Christianity, and they couldn't believe what they were seeing before their eyes, nor could they understand the level of unbelief and unchristian behaviour in the 'home of Christianity.' Naively they thought they'd be able to worship with their fellow Christians in Britain, as they belonged to the same church and were of 'one faith.' But it didn't quite work out that way. For a start, many West Indians were shocked at the attitude of British people to religion and church attendance. They were also surprised and many got a nasty shock when they turned up at their local church for Sunday Service, only to find that they were largely ignored, cold-shouldered, made to feel unwelcome, and some were even told not to come back as their presence was upsetting the white congregation. Because of this, many left the church and have never returned, while others were determined to stay, believing that the church was universal and belonged to everyone and not just to anyone race.

Ira Brooks, a pastor in the New Testament Church of God, describe to Anita Jackson, in her book, 'Catching Both Sides of the Wind,' his experience of visiting a Church of England for the first time, when he arrived in Britain.

When I got to Gloucester, I quickly sought out the Anglican church. I was a stranger and they offered nothing, absolutely nothing. Not that I was looking for anyone to lift me up but - I mean - a stranger in the country. Arriving with the warmth of the church I had known, I thought the church, especially the church, would have taken me in. Perhaps back home it was my local church where everybody knew everybody. I don't know. But here it was just a blank grey situation, just like the weather. Everything was cold. The people, the atmosphere. One of my first experiences was chilling. I discovered that certain pews in the church were reserved. How did I discover this? I went and took my seat, and then someone came up and politely hustled me away, drawing my attention to some name or number - I don't remember what was on the seat. And not being accustomed to English ways -you understand? - I had to think, I couldn't pick things up as quickly as they were saying them to me. I was partly bewildered. Sometimes it was days before you could interpret what happened last week. When I fully realised what this person was saying to me, that the seats were reserved, I went to sit at the back. After the service, nobody spoke to me.

Robinson Milward, now a Methodist minister in Stoke Newington, had a similar experience which he also related to Anita Jackson.

Yes, I have had negative experiences within the church. I would say that most of my experiences of racialism are not unique. They are the common experiences of my people. The depths of rejection I felt in the Methodist church when I came here. Think of a youngster just arrived in a foreign country, which you were taught was a Christian country, to be told by a minister with a dog-collar on his neck not to come back to his church. It was more than a bomb. I couldn't believe it. I went to his church where the congregation was white. I wasn't welcome because I was black. You'd be surprised how blunt people can be.

Not all West Indians felt rejected or were treated this way when they arrived in Britain. Rev Oliver Lyseight who in 1952 established the New Testament church of God in Wolverhampton, and Sybil Phoenix who came to Britain from Guyana in 1956 and a member of the Methodist church, both had an altogether different experience. Both were welcomed by their church, but they are the exception to the rule. The majority were shunned, ostracised, made to feel unwelcome, and made to feel that they didn't belong. For many years, this initial response by British Christians has strained the relationship between West Indian Christians and the Church of England, and it's only recently that the Church in England has officially acknowledged, and 'repented' of this folly and unchristian behaviour.

Pentecostal Christians reacted differently to the situation they found themselves in, and rather than try to fit in with the established church, sought out other Pentecostals and started to hold 'Prayer Meetings' in each other's homes. Many of the leaders were keen to keep the Pentecostal flame burning, as Dr S E Arnold in his book, 'From Scepticism to Hope' made clear:

'To prevent…. friends and fellow Christians, falling prey to the initial inertia that was rampant everywhere, [Pentecostal leaders] embarked on a militant plan to establish a fellowship to preserve their spiritual life, until they could return to the Caribbean.'

like the early Christians in the Bible, Pentecostals held their meetings in private so as not to attract attention, and because they were Pentecostals, they had a ready-made answer as to what was happening in Britain. For them it was a 'sign of the times' and signalled 'the coming of the Lord.' They therefore took comfort in the old West Indian chorus:

'Soon this life will all be over', with its refrain:

"Just a little while to stay here, just a little while to wait,' just a little while of troubles in this dark and sinful world."

PENTECOSTALISM

West Indian Pentecostals are part of a faith group that began in America around the 1890s and has its roots in the 'Holiness movement' of the 1900s. As a twentieth-century expression of Christianity, Pentecostalism is generally associated with the Azusa Street Revival of 1906 led by an African American, William Seymour. The Azusa Street Revival was a series of meetings which took place on April 9th at Azusa Street in Los Angeles California and lasted for eight years. Many Pentecostals today point to this event as the catalyst for the worldwide growth of Pentecostalism and the Charismatic movement. Theologically, Pentecostals stress several distinguishing features, one of which is 'speaking in tongues,' (glossolalia) which Pentecostals believes comes after conversion and water baptism. 'Speaking in tongues,' indicates that the believer has been filled/baptised in the 'holy spirit,' and in the 1920s, Pentecostalism found its way into Jamaica and the West Indies having been brought there by American missionaries. In the 1950s and 60s, when West Indians left for Britain, they took their Pentecostalism with them.

Pentecostalism isn't anything new in Britain as both the Elim Church and the Assemblies of God, -both Pentecostal churches- pre-date the arrival of West Indian Christians and have been around since the 1900s. What's not clear is whether they made any overtures to their fellow Christians, when West Indians arrived in Britain. It's unlikely that they did, for if they did, there'd be anecdotal evidence in the Black community about this. What I do know is on an individual level there were, because one of my father's minister -elder

Chadwick who remained with him for many years, came from a White Pentecostal Church tradition. Also, another was Pastor Jones from Wales, and I remember in the summer months, we as a church would make regular trips to join him and his small congregation in South Wales. Besides, at various Black Pentecostal services, it wasn't unusual to see the odd white Christian, who may have come from this church tradition.

PRAYER MEETINGS

West Indian first expression of worship in Britain were *'Prayer Meetings.'* These were 'church services' held in a person's home after work, usually on a Wednesday or Friday evening. *Prayer Meetings'* followed a simple format. The meeting would start with some singing (mainly choruses), followed by *'testimonies.'* A short sermon would be next, and the meeting would end with an 'altar call.' (more about this later). Once the 'Prayer Meeting was over, refreshments were always served, and this could either be a simple snack or a full-blown meal. 'Prayer Meetings,' gave West Indians a chance to give their 'testimonies' affirming their faith, as well as an opportunity to share their experiences of living and working in Britain. It also provided an opportunity for anyone to publicly thank God for 'all He had done,' and for West Indians, thanking God is everything. They thanked Him for getting a job, a pay rise, a new family member arriving from 'home,' or for receiving healing. West Indians believed that:

'In Everything Give Thanks'......
(I Thessalonians 5:18-King James Version)

Once the testimony part of the meeting was over, the next stage was 'bringing the word,' or 'delivering the message'. 'Bringing the word' is Pentecostal speak for a short sermon which either the pastor or one of the senior members in the meeting would give. A sermon in this setting is simply an exposition of a bible verse, a passage of scripture or a bible story which the pastor explains showing how each person should apply its meaning to both their natural and spiritual life.

With the sermon over, the altar call' comes next. This in a *prayer meeting* is an invitation to anyone who is not 'born again,' *(not saved, or a Christian)* to be given a chance to do so. A person indicates this by raising their hand during this part of the service, and with this 'indication' they are prayed for and 'receive Christ.' The meeting then ends with the singing of a hymn, a final prayer and the 'doxology.' The 'doxology' which is now hardly ever heard, was once a feature of all West Indian Worship. It's roughly equivalent to the 'blessing' in an Anglican service, although, in a West Indian church, the doxology could either be said or sung.

"Praise God from whom all blessings flow, Praise Him all creatures here below, Praise Him above ye, heavenly host, praise Father, Son and Holy Ghost.'

In the early years, *prayer meetings* worked well for West Indians and as more and more people arrived, and as their numbers grew, a network of meetings sprang up all over the country. Soon *prayer meetings* were everywhere in West Indian communities, and with it the embryonic structure of the Black Pentecostal church in Britain began to take shape. Sunday Services were soon added and these were usually held in a pastor's house, or in one of the senior member's house who had managed to buy a house by then.

SUNDAY SERVICES

Each Sunday, West Indians gathered in their Pastor's front room to hold their services. The room was often set out to look like a small chapel, with rows of chairs on either side of the room and a passageway down the middle. A small table at the front would act as the alter, as well as it was from there that the pastor conducted the service. On the table was always a vase of freshly cut flowers, a jug of water, two drinking glass, the offering plate, and a small bottle of olive oil would complete the setting. Why the olive oil? It was used to 'anoint' - rub a small spot on the forehead- when praying for the sick.

is anyone among you sick? Let him call for the elders of the church, and let them pray over him, anointing him with oil in the name of the Lord. (James 5:14)

Both *Prayer Meetings* and Sunday Services were every bit a West Indian Christian experience and both were places where West Indian went to worship, meet and make friends, hear news from home, and as a community, there was always someone on hand to help with any official matters. Many of today's Black Pentecostal church started this way, including *The Church of God in Christ* in 1952 at 57 Navarino Road in Hackney East London, *The New Testament Church of God* in 1953 in Wolverhampton, *The Church of God of Prophecy* in the same year, Bethel United Church of Jesus Christ (Apostolic) in 1955, *The Seventh Day Adventist church, The New Testament Assembly* in the 1960s, and my own father's church at 77 Berriman Road in North London in 1953.

THE MOVE TO CHURCH HALLS

Both *Prayer Meetings* and *Sunday Services* became popular in West Indian communities, and it was soon obvious that larger premises were needed to accommodate the growing number of people wishing to attend these services. Once again, West Indians found themselves, confronting the same problem they once faced, as they looked for halls to hold their services. The idea this time was to approach local parishes to see if they would help, as they tended to have suitable halls, but many were reluctant fearing loss of respectability, and because many had never done this before, they were therefore unwilling.

It might appear simple now but then it was tough trying to find a suitable place to hold a church service, and if a hall was found it was one mainly used at weekend for local dances and general entertainment. On many occasions when West Indians turned up to hold their church service, they were often met with a dirty hall which they had to first clean out and then they had the problem of putting up with the smell of stale alcohol and tobacco, that lingered throughout the service.

In the winter month's they had another problem. Many of these halls, were always cold with very little heating, and if there were any, they were usually small inefficient gas heaters inadequate for the size of the room, or the number of people in it. As a result, during the winter months, many West Indians held their services in cold buildings which seemed only to get warm by the time they were leaving. However, despite all this, hardly anyone complained, for they were thankful they had somewhere to worship in the manner they were used to.

'OPEN AIR SERVICES'

From the beginning, West Indians placed a great emphasis on evangelism, especially street evangelism, and they would hold regular street or 'open-air services' both as a 'witness' and as a way of attracting members to their churches. 'Open-air services' were mainly held on Saturday afternoons near to markets where West Indians shopped, or on busy street corners. These 'open-air' events were a shortened version of an actual church service with plenty of music, singing, playing the tambourine, and church members would give out 'handouts' *(leaflets-flyers)* to shoppers and passers-by. Crucially they'd have the church address and times of service printed on the back, to encourage shoppers to attend the church.

I must have been about eight or nine when I started to follow my father to many of his 'open-air services'. I would play my accordion to accompany the singing while he did the preaching. Because of my age and as a small Black boy in those days playing an accordion, I attracted quite a bit of attention. Obviously, I didn't appreciate this at the time, but my father did, and would regularly wheel me out to play at these and other church services which he held or attended.

In the 1960s, 'open-air services' were not unusual in Britain as the Salvation Army and other church denominations held them regularly. Donald Soper - the celebrated Methodist minister and Noble Peer was famous for his open-air preaching which he did every Wednesday for over 40 years at Tower Bridge and every Sunday at 'Speakers Corner' in central London. When I was in my teens, I would regularly go after church to 'Speaker's Corner' to see 'free speech' in action. This was the beginning of my political education and where it began to take root. Many times I would listen to Donald Soper, political speakers, complete mad hatters, hecklers, eccentrics and an array of minor orators, all trying to get their points across in the place George Orwell once described as, "one of the minor wonders of the world."

Apart from 'open-air services,' one of the defining features of West Indian churches in the 1960s, was their strong sense of community. Churches were not only places of worship but were also places where anyone could meet, make friends and where people cared for and looked after each other. They were also places where West Indians bought their problems and expected to have their spiritual and social needs met. Even a pastor's role at this time extended beyond the church and out into the wider community, and although most pastors had a full-time job, they'd be expected to provide help and support to anyone in need. Many times, my father, often at nights, would be called out into the community to pray for a sick, and when needed, provide a word of comfort, or help someone in need. In the daytime, unsupported financially, he would also do the same and if he found anyone in need, he would bring them home, and they would be assured of a cup of tea, some West Indian hospitality, and the word of God!

Churches during the early years were also places where West Indians could go after a week working in what was often an 'hostile environment', and immerse themselves in West Indian worship, culture, language and practices, reinforcing not only who they were as Christians but also who they were as West Indians. The church also provided the strength West Indians needed and could draw from, and they would often hear from the pulpit or as part of a testimony, a range of strategies to employ in their everyday battles, especially when they faced racism in society or in the work place.

As for young people, West Indian churches provided a shield against all that was going on in society, allowing them to grow in character and self worth. It gave them a sense of identity, provided a moral compass for them to live by, and gave them the resolve to face life as a Black person from a position of strength, rather than from one that was weak, confused, or insecure. Churches were also both sacred and social places and were the soil in which the first Black Pentecostal church took root, and from where it has since grown and developed.

A WEST INDIAN CHURCH SERVICE

Once a group of West Indians had found a hall to rent, they held their services in the way they liked, according to their custom and in a manner, they were used to. Culturally their *liturgy* was what they had brought with them from the West Indies, and they practised it as far as they could in Britain. As an example, a typical Jamaican Pentecostal service starts with '*Sunday School*,' which in the early days meant, everyone in the congregation as there weren't enough children to separate into classes. Generally, a female member leads this part of the service, usually someone who was once a teacher 'back home.' The highlight of '*Sunday School*' was always, 'reciting the golden text' or the memory verse which everyone was expected to do. 'Reciting the golden text' always bought a great deal of laughter, as the older members in the church whose reading wasn't particularly good, struggled to remember what they had tried to commit to memory.

Once Sunday School was over, the next stage is the *Devotional Service*, which is the formal part of the worship and generally begins with the singing of some '*lively choruses*,' which are up-tempo songs. Choruses were once popular in West Indian churches and although many of them are not heard today, they were formerly the mainstay of West Indian singing and worship. To get a sense of what they might have sounded like,

Donnie McClurkin's *'Caribbean Medley'* on his *'Live in London'* CD-[11] is a good example and comes very close. (more about this later)

Some typical West Indian choruses are:

'Born, Born, Born Again thank
God I'm born again.'

'Let the fire fall on me.'

'Hide Me Under the Blood.'

West Indians sang choruses all the time in their services, and even in the winter months when they struggled in halls that were cold and uninviting, they would always sing this chorus, *'It is summertime in my heart'* as if to warm both body and soul.

It is summertime down in my heart.
It is summertime down in my heart.
When Jesus Saved me, new life He gave me
And when it's winter, It's summer down in my heart.'-

HYMNS featured prominently in West Indian services which is a throwback to the influence of the Anglican church in the West Indies. Most hymns came from, *Hymns Ancient and Modern* which was introduced in Jamaica in 1861 and remained there for many years. In Europe, hymns took a long time to be accepted and before the seventeenth century, congregational singing wasn't allowed in churches because of the stranglehold the Catholic church had on the music. Any singing had to come directly from the bible, otherwise, it was an 'error of popery,' and therefore banned. The aristocracy however could get professional musicians to perform hymns for them in their private chapels.[12]

The German Monk and theologian, Martin Luther had a different idea on hymns, and in his writings encouraged churches in Germany to sing hymns in their own language rather than in Latin, much to the annoyance and displeasure of the Catholic church. Luther loved music and knew the power of it.

Next to the word of God, music deserves the highest praise. She is a mistress and governess of those human emotions...... which control men... or more often overwhelm them.....Whether you wish to comfort the sad, subdue frivolity, to encourage the departing, to humble the proud, to calm the passionate, or to appease those full of hate...what more effective means than music could you find? [13]

Apart from hymns, Luther was also critical of the Catholic church and the hold it had on people and made this plain in his writings. Helped by the printing press, his ideas spread widely in Europe and for this, he was excommunicated, but not before, in the period known as the *Reformation*, he had helped to loosen the stranglehold the Catholic Church had on people's lives.

One of the first moves towards hymn singing in Britain came with the hymns of Benjamin Keach, a Baptist minister who in 1673, encouraged his congregation in Southwark South London to sing a hymn after communion as an example of what Jesus disciples did at the end of the Last Supper- [14]

'And when they had sung a hymn, they went out into the Mount of Olives' – Matthew 26: 30

Of all the hymn writers, Isaac Watts (1674-1748) is perhaps the best known. He did a lot to popularise hymn singing, and in the eighteenth century, his hymns were popular in England. He wrote over 600 hymns, including, *'Joy to the world, 'Oh God our help in ages past, When I survey the wondrous cross,' Come ye that love the Lord etc.* Watts Hymns and Spiritual Songs were well known in America and they found a special place in the hearts of the American slaves who took to them, and Watts hymns, in turn, influenced their music, *the spirituals.* Both John and Charles Wesley the founder of the Methodist church, had a similar effect, as did John Newton-the former slave trader, who wrote: *Amazing Grace.*

The story behind *Amazing Grace*, is that abandoned in West Africa, and eventually rescued by slave traders, Newton himself became a trader between London and West Africa. On one of his trips back to Britain, Newton's ship was engaged in a violent storm, and fearing he would die, vowed that if God spared his life he would abandon life as a slave trader and work in the service of the church. Once home, Newton changed his life, became an Anglican priest, a hymn writer and a lifelong supporter of William Wilberforce and the abolitionists who were fighting to end the slave trade. It was during this period that he wrote *Amazing Grace,* his great hymn of conversion.

Amazing grace! how sweet the sound, that saved a wretch; like me! once was lost, but now am found, was blind, but now I see.

Although the Church of God of Prophecy and the Seventh Day Adventist had their own hymn books when they came to

Britain, all other West Indians churches hymns, came from one of two books, 'Sacred Songs and Solos', by Ira D. Sankey, published in 1873, and 'The Redemption Hymnal' published in 1951 by the Elim Pentecostal Church.

'TRACKING A HYMN' is a style of singing which West Indians used in their services as it allowed everyone to join in the singing, whether they could read or not, or whether they had a hymnbook or not. 'Tracking a hymn' has long been associated with America where it's called 'lining.' It's thought to have originated in Scotland, taken to the Southern States of America, and in 1780, found its way to Jamaica. 'Tracking a hymn' is when a member of a congregation reads out loud, line by line, the words of a hymn as it's being sung, and with this, the congregation joins in, singing each line simultaneously. The hymn continues this way until it is finished.

"a [person] would chant each line, and the congregation would repeat that line; before the congregation would finish the first line, the [person] would start the second line in time for the congregation to start that second line and so on until the song was completed." [15]

CHORUSES are the mainstay of West Indian church music, and an essential aide-memoire. When in a service a chorus is 'raised,' (*starts*) the whole congregation joins in, singing in their own harmonies, swaying, clapping their hands and spiritually letting go in the process. Choruses came out of the *'Great Revival'* tradition in America in the 1850s, when after a series of economic, social and political failures, the country 'turned to God in a time of mass prayer meetings, repentance and spiritual renewal'. In 1851, this sense of spiritual awareness, reached Jamaica and there the songs and religious expression of the *'Great Revival,'* fused with the music and African beliefs of the indigenous Jamaicans, and out of this, the Jamaican Revivalist music tradition was born - singing, drumming, dancing, handclapping, foot-stomping, and groaning. Jamaican Pentecostals adopted many of these practices, and the choruses West Indians brought to Britain, came out of this tradition.

West Indians love to sing choruses, and it is in the singing of them that the distinct identity of West Indian church music finds its true expression, a mixture of pathos and transcendent joy, when congregation, voice, instruments, hand clapping, feet stomping and tambourine playing becomes ONE, in a unique moment of praise to God. Joel Edwards, in his book, *'Let's Praise Him Again,'* describe choruses as: songs that,

"incorporate a bold simplicity and urgency, conveyed by repetitive and uncompromising directness."

James Baldwin in *'The Fire Next Time'* say that:

'There's no music like the music, no drama like the drama of the saints rejoicing, the sinner moaning, the tambourines racing, and all those voices coming together and crying holy unto the Lord'.

SCRIPTURE READING is part of every church service, and in West Indian worship, it mainly comes from the Old Testament in the King James version. The reading is done, *'alternatively,'* which means that the person doing the reading, reads out one verse at a time, after which the congregation responds by reading the next or *alternate verse.* This continues until the penultimate verse, when everyone joins in, reading the last verse together. The reading usually ends with the *'Gloria Patri,'*-

'Glory be to the Father and to the Son and to the holy ghost. As it was in the beginning, it's now and forever shall be, world without end amen-.'

In some cases in West Indian services, after the scripture reading, the next part, is a *'time of testimonies,'* but this is unusual, for *testimonies* are usually reserved for the evening service, where it features and is the highlight. However, if a person is *'called on'* (asked) or volunteer to give a *testimony*, it's likely to follow along these lines:

"Shall we praise the Lord?"

The congregation raises their hands and respond, *"Praise the Lord,"*
'Let's praise Him again saints! says the person giving the testimony to emphasise the point. This may be repeated several times until the whole congregation is paying attention and a *'spiritual connection,'* has been made.

They, then continue:

"*First giving honour to God*, the person would say, after which they'd greet all the ministers, naming all of them one by one, and after what is sometimes an elaborate introduction, the person then shares their experience (*testimony*) of living and working in Britain, often citing something good which had happened to them in the past week and thanking God for it. If there was something unpleasant, they'd share this also, crucially citing how the Lord had helped them to overcome whatever it was, and if they'd not been able to do so, they'd ask for prayer to help them.

'OVERCOMING THINGS' was especially important to West Indian Christians, as they saw life as a constant struggle, and believed that it is only with the help of God, they are able to 'overcome' things. Their testimony was their way of showing this and publicly thanking God for helping them to do so.

'PRAY WITHOUT CEASING' is what the bible says, and West Indian Christians took this literally, not saying prayers, for that's too passive. Praying they believe is an active imperative, and nothing was off-limits when it came to praying. Even mundane things like praying for a bus to arrive wasn't unusual, or someone to call, or bring a *word from the Lord*. In the early days, prayer was especially important, and whether it was in a prayer meeting, a church service or a chance meeting, West Indians would always appeal for prayer or seek an opportunity to do so. They would ask for prayer for themselves, for their family, for a job, prayer to resolve a difficult situation, for a personal need, or prayer for healing. In fact, the usual refrain when two West Indian Pentecostals were about to leave each other's company was, *'You pray for me and I'll pray for you.'* Prayer was everything, it was a West Indian Christian life force as it showed their total and absolute dependence on God.

All this and more were part of a West Indian prayer regime, and in their churches, praying is a collective experience and one, where everyone, prays as an individual and collectively. It's wonderful to hear a congregation of hundreds of West Indians praying at the same time and hearing the collective sound they make. As a child, I loved the sound and used to wonder how God heard all these prayers, let alone every individual one.

Congregational prayer can take a long time, as there's no limit when it should end. Churches, however, have a few tricks up their sleeves to signal to a congregation that they should bring their collective praying to an end. One way is that one of the leaders usually says loudly a few times, *'Amen, Amen,'* when its time to bring the praying to an end, and you can bet at this point one voice would suddenly rise to the top as the other voices are dying down, 'taking the floor' as it were, and praying for a few minutes more so that everyone can hear. A collective Amen by all, finally brings the praying to an end.

COLLECTING THE OFFERING- (The offertory) usually follows testimonies and this in turn is followed by the 'notices' after which, the choir or a soloist may be asked to sing. If it's the choir, they would make their way to the front of the church and sing a *'special rendition'* or number that they had previously prepared. After this, the pastor, *'brings the word'* or *'deliver the message,'* in other words, preach the sermon

SERMONS in West Indian services were always without notes, rousing and theatrical and often came from the Old Testament. They were the highlight of a service and could last for a long time, sometimes up to two hours. They were often 'end time' messages, apocalyptic, with emphasis on *holiness, repentance, heaven and hell.* At regular intervals, the congregation would shout, *'Amen,' 'Praise the Lord,' 'Glory', 'Hallelujah,'* in a *'call and response'* manner, affirming what the preacher was saying.

'ALTAR CALL,' ends all West Indian services, and this is an invitation to everyone who is not *'saved'* or *'born-again'*, to have a chance to do so. The congregation usually sing some mournful songs at this point to reinforce the seriousness of the occasion, as well as to *'invoke a sense of dread.'* If a person indicated that they wanted to be *saved*, they'd walk to the front, (the altar) where they'd be prayed for and *'receive Christ'.*

An Altar call is always a life and death decision which everyone in a West Indian service is expected to make. The preacher during altar calls often repeats several times *'choose life, not death'*, *'come and be saved,'* as if to reinforce this point. This is repeated until the preacher is satisfied that everyone has had a chance to decide. When this is done, anyone who went to the front was prayed for, and a couple of church sisters would be expected to follow up with them after the service.

There are some choice songs which were part of every *Altar Call* and were always heard at this point. They included, *'There were ninety and nine,'* with its imagery of the lost sheep. Another was, *'Alas and did my Saviour bleed,'* and *'Oh, Happy Day that fixed my choice.'* The latter was also sung at baptismal services, and in 1968 it became a worldwide hit, as, *'Oh Happy Day,'* for the Edwin Hawkins Singers.

With the *Altar Call* over, the congregation sings a final hymn, a person is asked to pray, and the service comes to an end with the singing of the *'doxology.'* Within a few hours, they'd all be back again for the evening service, where this time, the *'testimony service'* dominates and is the highlight.

MOVE TO PERMANENT BUILDINGS

West Indian services were always an extended affair and could last for hours. In rented halls, churches soon came up against many restrictions including the length of their services. This and the rate at which they were growing, made them realise they needed their own buildings and they set about raising the money to do so. They came up with many fund-raising ideas, including, staging *'building programme events, concerts, 'rallies,' and pledges*, which is where a member promises a certain amount of money towards buying the church. Then, there was always the ever-present *pardner* to help in this process, and with this collective effort, it wasn't long before many West Indians had their own places of worship. Soon their churches became the focal point of their communities, providing places where people could meet socially, worship, get married, have their babies *blessed,'* (christened), as well as places, they could hold their funeral services.

How many Black Pentecostal churches were purchased at this time is unknown, but what we do know is that the churches that began in people's homes in the 1950s, including, *'The Church of God in Christ', 'The New Testament Church of God', 'The Church of God of Prophecy', Bethel United Church of Jesus Christ (Apostolic), The New Testament Assembly* and my own father's church, are all still going today, and are now very much part of the British religious landscape.

THE FIRST WEST INDIAN CHURCHES IN BRITAIN

The Church of God in Christ (COGIC)

The church that can lay claim to be the first Black Caribbean Pentecostal church in Britain, and which established Black Pentecostal worship in the country, is the Church of God in Christ (COGIC) - the oldest Caribbean church. COGIC is a famous Black American Pentecostal church which was founded by Bishop Charles H Mason in Mississippi in 1907. Charles Mason was an ordained Baptist minister in Arkansas, and in 1906 travelled to Los Angeles to participate in the Azusa Street Revival led by William Seymour. Inspired by what he saw and heard there, Mason returned to Arkansas, and in 1907 along with a group of cotton pickers, sharecroppers, domestic servants, and ex-slaves, started the Church of God in Christ. In 1925 the church moved to Memphis Tennessee where it has remained ever since, and on the completion of its headquarters in 1940, renamed the building, Mason Temple, in recognition of its founder Charles Mason.

Today COGIC is a well-known and famous church in America within the African American tradition. It has an estimated worldwide membership of 8 million people, and over 12,000 churches. In 1968, on the night before he was assassinated, Dr Martin Luther King preached his famous *'I've been to the mountain top'* sermon in Mason Temple, and in 1965 Malcolm X funeral service was also held at a COGIC church in Harlem. What is not generally known, is that Sarah Palin -remember her? - is a member of COGIC, and that the mostly white Assemblies of God church, was once a member of the Church of God in Christ! [16]

The British branch of the church of God in Christ, started in 1952 as a prayer meeting in the home of Mrs Mary McLachlan, at 57 Navarino Road in Hackney North London. Both my parents knew mother and bishop McLachlan as they were both former members of the Church of God in Christ. I vaguely remember her, more because she was a friend of my mother, whereas Bishop McLachlan was a bit more detached. 'Mother McLachlan,' as she was affectionately known, came to Britain from Jamaica in the 1950s and unable to find a Pentecostal church in London, gathered a few friends and together they started to hold prayer meetings in her home.

In the same year, Bishop Charles H Mason the head of the Church in America came to Britain to attend, 'The World Pentecostal Conference' at Westminster Central Hall in London. He heard about a small group of Black Pentecostals in the capital and sought them out. It was this meeting that eventually led Mother McLachlan to join with Bishop Mason and established a branch of his Church in Britain. Once back in America, Bishop Mason sent over to Britain Mrs White a member of his church to help Mother McLachlan with the church in London. Mother McLachlan warmly received her and together the two women set about growing the church, moving it from Mother McLachlan's front room, to a rented hall in Sussex Gardens, in Brixton.

At first, Pentecostals arriving from the West Indies, joined the church in London because it was the only one, but as more and more came, some joined Mother McLachlan, while others started their own 'prayer meetings' or joined existing ones in the capital. Some of the early names associated with the COGIC church in London and later went on to become well-known names within the early West Indian church community are, Elder Payne, Elder Marsh, Elder Edwards, Elder Campbell and my own father, Elder Francis as he was known then.

In 1954 Mother McLachlan's husband, Bishop Oswald McLachlan came to Britain and took over the running of the church. From Sussex Gardens, Bishop and Mother McLachlan went on to establish another branch in Camden Town North London. Three years later, both Bishop and Mother McLachlan went to Memphis to attend the Church of God in Christ international Convention, and it was while there that the relationship between Bishop McLachlan and the church in Britain was formalised, with Bishop McLachlan appointed, Overseer of the church in London.

During its formative years, COGIC moved several times and went through several crises. One of these caused severe disruption and almost split the church. The problem I understand was a disagreement between Bishop McLachlan in London and Bishop Ashmead who had started a branch of the church in Luton. Back from a visit to the church in Memphis, Ashmead claimed that while there, he was appointed the overall Bishop of the church in Britain! This led to an obvious clash between McLachlan and Ashmead, and unable to reconcile their differences, the two leaders decided to part and go their separate ways. Not long after, Ashmead branch of the church disbanded, and Bishop McLachlan was left in sole charge of the church of God in Christ in Britain.

In 1963, Bishop McLachlan announced that he was returning to Jamaica because of ill health, but before he left, he appointed Bishop Clifford Bell as the National Overseer, the post, Bell held until his death in 1998.

Under the leadership of Bishop Bell, the church moved again but this time to a Methodist Church hall in Richmond Road in North London where it remained for several years. The church grew steadily but not as much as it had done in the early years when it was the main Pentecostal church in Britain. The reasons for the decline are varied and complex but undoubtedly one of the explanations is the emergence of 'The Church of God of Prophecy' and the 'New Testament Church of God' in the late 1960s. Both these churches have strong links in Jamaica, and when their members started coming to Britain, rather than go to a COGIC church, they now had their own church to go to. By the late 1970s, both churches had eclipsed COGIC as the dominant player in the Black Pentecostal church community in Briain. Today, the Church of God in Christ is a shadow of its former self, but it is once again on the rise, led by Bishop Alvin Blake who ironically has moved the headquarters of the church from London, to a multi-church complex, in the heart of Luton.

The New Testament Church of God

The New Testament church of God -was originally named, *'The Church of God'* and was established in America in 1886. It is one of the oldest Black Pentecostal church in the country, and today it is an international organisation with a global reach. The British section of the church was started in 1953 in Wolverhampton by its founder Oliver Rev A Lyseight. Lyseight was a member of the New Testament Church of God in Jamaica. He was born in 1919 in Claremont Hanover, the fourth of 12 children. At the age of 27, he started his ministry, and after spending some time in America, arrived in Britain in 1952.

Lyseight experience of the established church in Britain is different from what others felt. While many West Indian Christians were ignored by their local church, Lyseight said that when he first went to Darlington Street Methodist church in Wolverhampton, he found 'a warm welcome there'. Things however changed with the arrival of a new minister, and he decided to leave. Leyseight gathered a few Christian friends together and started to hold prayer meetings in his home. From there they moved to a YMCA hall in the centre of town, and on the 20th of September 1953, with his group of worshipers, Leyseight held his first service there.

While Leyseight was starting a church in Wolverhampton, another group of like-minded Christians were also meeting in Handsworth Birmingham. They were led by Pastor G A Johnson, and when Lyseight got to hear of Johnson and his group of worshippers, he left Wolverhampton to visit them. It wasn't long before Leyseight and Johnson joined, and they set about growing the New Testament Church of God in Britain from its base in the Midlands. In 1955 Lyseight was appointed National Overseer with Johnson his deputy. Together they put administrative structures in place, set up regional offices, purchase church buildings, and as the church expanded, established training institutions also. In 2006, at the age of 86, Lyseight died, and on the 60th Anniversary of The New Testament Church of God, a Blue Plaque was unveiled in the city of Wolverhampton in recognition of his work as the first leader of the New Testament Church of God in Britain, and also for his service to the local community. Today the New Testament Church of God is the largest Black Pentecostal Caribbean church in Britain, with over 11,000 registered members, around 40,000 adherents, 108 pastors and 120 congregations and missions.[17]

The Pentecostal Church of the First Born.

My own father's church started life in 1953, in the front room of our house at 77 Berriman Road North London. My father first worked on the railways laying 'sleepers,' and on the recommendation of a friend, Elder Edwards who had arrived earlier in Britain, started worshipping at the fledgling church of God in Christ in Camden Town North London. He remained there for three years but in 1956 decided to strike out on his own. From Berriman Road, my father moved to a rented church hall in upper Holloway Road which is near to the Archway in Islington London. The church grew steadily, when in 1963, he moved again to another church hall, this time in Richmond Avenue in Islington. The church experienced remarkable growth during this time and held regular packed meetings, weeklong conventions, rallies, and many evangelistic healing services. At one time the church was known as, *'The Deliverance Centre'* because of a decisive turn my father took in his ministry. This came after my mother was diagnosed with terminal cancer, and through prayer, fasting and the support of the church, was miraculously healed.

In 1967 the church moved from Richmond Avenue to its own premises at 71 White lion street Islington which it bought at a time when most West Indian churches were still worshipping in rented halls. With its own premises, my father's church grew along with his ministry, and at one time he had churches in London, Birmingham, Hitchin, Henlow, Luton and several in America and Jamaica.

Like many West Indian ministers, in the early years my father made frequent trips to America. He was influenced by what he saw there, and when we bought a Hammond Organ (the first church in Britain to do so), the style of worship changed. Before long, we were known as the 'American church,' because of the American influence on our music, singing and style of worship.

In the 1970s my father took another decisive step. Over the years he had developed a relationship with a church in Waycross Georgia who several times invited him over to preach. Out of these visits grew a close relationship and in 1979, he decided to throw in his lot with the church in Georgia. Since then, our church was the UK branch of the church in America. I remember when the Inspirational choir was promoting their first single, the record company liked the long name of the church and used it as a marketing ploy. Radio DJs would fall over themselves trying to read out the full name of the choir, *the inspirational choir of the Pentecostal First Born Church of the Living God*, and do so, without crashing into the start of the choir's track they had on their turntable!

Today, both my parents have since died, and the church now in its 67th year is led by bishop Fairin, with the headquarters moved to Birmingham. It has since changed its name again, and today is known as, *The International Church of the Firstborn of the Living God.*

The Church of God of Prophecy

The second-largest Black Pentecostal church in Britain is The Church of God of Prophecy. The church was started in 1886 by A.J. Tomlinson in Cherokee County, North Carolina. In 1903 it relocated to Cleveland Tennessee, where it was formally recognised as the Church of God. After a series of litigation, the Church adopted the name, The Church of God of Prophecy, and today it has over one-and-a-half million members, with over 10,000 churches, located in over 125 countries. The Church of God of Prophecy started in Britain in 1953 when A.J. Tomlinson sent his son Homer to Britain to start a church there. While in the country Homer met Herbert White an Englishman, and together along with thirteen members, they started to meet as a church in Bedford. [18]

At first, this was essentially a white member church but as West Indians began arriving in Britain in the 1960s, many of whom were already members of the church of God of Prophecy in the West Indies, especially in Jamaica, they got to hear of the church in Bedford and went there to worship. It wasn't long however before the complexion of the church began to change, and this led to a great deal of uneasiness among the white members. There was also another problem. It centred on the wearing of jewellery, including a wedding ring, which the main church in America was against but the church in Britain was ambivalent about. The scripture most cited to support this was, I Peter 3:3:

Whose adorning let it not be that outward adorning of plaiting the hair, and of wearing gold, or of putting on of apparel.

The white members in the church in Bedford were more liberal about *wearing gold, or putting on apparel,* unlike the West Indians who were traditional and orthodox in their approach. The tension this generated merely added to the on-going difficulties between the two groups, and as a result, many of the white members left to join another, (white) Church of God of Prophecy in the area.

As more West Indians arrived and settled in Britain, they started branches of their own church of God of Prophecy in their own areas. Soon the Church became a predominantly Black Caribbean one. The *'mother church'* in America couldn't ignore what was happening and after a shaky start, threw its weight behind the church and began to fully support it. After all, the church in Britain was bringing it international prestige, as well as being a valuable asset.

Today, the church of God of Prophecy is in many of the major towns and cities in Britain where Caribbean people live, and although in recent years its membership has been in decline, mainly because of its ageing population, it still, has around 4000 members, with 63 churches and 251 ministries.[19]

Bethel United Church of Jesus Christ-Apostolic

Bethel United church – formally First United Church of Jesus Christ, Apostolic, is the main 'Oneness' Pentecostal church in Britain. In West Indian church circles, people from this church tradition are known as, 'Jesus Only' because they baptise their members, *'In the name of Jesus'* whereas, traditional Pentecostal churches, baptise, theirs, *'in the name of the father, son and holy ghost'.* Theologically, Apostolic have moved away from the mainstream Christian doctrine of the Trinity- *(father, son and holy ghost)* as they believe that there is only one person in the Godhead - *Jesus Christ.*

Historically, the 'Oneness church' started in America around the 1900s as part of the Pentecostal movement. They were once part of the Assemblies of God but broke away to form their own denomination. Dunn a member of the 'oneness' church in Jamaica, arrived in Britain in 1955, and unable to find a 'oneness' church, decided to start one of his own. In the same year his fiancé Chloe Thompson, arrived from Jamaica to join him, and they married; beginning a 50 years relationship in which she worked with him in establishing the church in Britain.

Like most West Indian church leaders, Dunn began his church as a series of 'prayer meetings' which he held in his home. He moved several times after that, finally ending up at Lozells Road in the west part of Birmingham. A dispute arose with the group and Dunn left. He found a building at 2 Gibson road, purchased it, and started a church there, where it has remained ever since.

For 55 years, Dunn grew the church and the Apostolic tradition in Caribbean circles in Britain, and by the time of his death in 2017, he had established 42 churches across the UK, with others in Liberia, America, Canada and Jamaica. Dunn's greatest physical legacy is the 2,500 purpose-built, Bethel church and convention centre at West Bromwich in Birmingham, which today stands as a great monument to him and his legacy.

The Seventh Day Adventist (SDA)

The Seventh-day Adventist Church is a Protestant denomination and its main distinguishing feature is Saturday as the Sabbath and not Sunday. As a religious movement, The Seventh-day Adventists began in America in 1863 as part of the early Millerite movement, whose leader, William Miller, predicted that the world would end in 1843 and that Christ would return to earth as the second advent. Among his followers, was, Ellen Gould White, whose visions and 'revelations' have guided the church until her death in 1915. Today the Seventh-day Adventist church is a worldwide organisation with an estimated membership of up to 40 million people.

During the early years, Seventh Day Adventists were not numerically strong in the West Indies, and when their members arrived in Britain, they looked for Adventists churches to worship in. Because of the demand of their faith, they could hardly go elsewhere. For example, the Seventh Day Adventists observe and celebrate the Sabbath, the seventh day of the week if you count Sunday as the first day, or the seventh day of creation, and as such it would have been difficult for them to go anywhere else other than to an Adventist church.

At first, the church in Britain was predominantly white, but as more and more West Indian Adventists began arriving in the 1960s, the profile of the church began to change. Many White members felt threatened by this and left, but the number of West Indians continued to rise inexorably.

Out of the 16,000 Adventists in British churches, a minimum of 65%, probably more, are of Afro-Caribbean origin. Some churches are 100% black and black-led. About 27 of the 75 or so pastors are Afro Caribbean (about 36%). Although the overall numbers in the Church have risen markedly since the beginning of Afro-Caribbean immigration there has been a steady exodus of white people from Adventism. As numbers of Afro-Caribbean's increased, numbers of white members decreased. [20]

This tension between white and black in the Seventh-day Adventist Church once led people to describe it as a 'white-led Black Church.' In the 1970s the issue of Black representation in the Seventh Day Adventists leadership was serious enough to almost cause a schism. A solution was found and agreed on which saw provisions made for African-Caribbean pastors in churches where the African Caribbean are in the majority. Therefore, the notion now that the Seventh Day Adventist is a white led church with a Black membership, is not entirely true, for not all ministers are white, and not all the members are Black. There are Black pastors today in churches where there is a Black majority and there is Black representation in most departments of the church. There are also Black Adventists in senior positions, and the current President of the church in Britain and Ireland is Black.

The New Testament Assembly

The New Testament Assembly was founded by Bishop Melvin Powell along with his sister I O Smith, Bishop Bernard, and Alfred Doyley. Born in Portland Jamaica in 1931, Bishop Powell was ordained a minister in the New Testament Assembly church, and it was while pastoring there that he met Donald Bernard who became a lifelong friend. Together when they arrived in Britain in the 1960s, they set about establishing a branch of the church in Tooting South London.

A pastor in the New Testament Assembly in Jamaica, Bishop Powell as he later became known, left Jamaica in 1940 to travel to America to work as a farm labourer as part of the country's foreign worker's scheme. He worked in several states, and while there, enrolled at the Cleveland Bible College in Tennessee, where he studied for a Diploma in theology.

On his return to Jamaica, Melvin met Amey Rose and in 1956 they were married. Along with a young wife, Melvin continued to work in the church and took his ministry across the Island. In 1961 he decided like many of his contemporaries to travel to Britain in search of work and to seek out new opportunities for him and his young family. The intention was to stay for only a short time, and when his long-time friend Donald Bernard arrived, with a handful of friends, they started a branch of the New Testament Assembly in the front room of a house in Tooting South London. Along with Donald Bernard who by now was ordained a bishop as well, Powell and Bernard grew the church, so that by the time Bishop Powell died in 2008 they were responsible for churches in Jamaica, USA, Canada, India, Ghana and South Africa, with several branches in Britain including the headquarters in Tooting South London.

Bishop Powell was a humble man and with foresight, set out a financial plan for the New Testament Assembly, which saw it purchase several church properties, placing it in good stead and making it financially secure. The church also works within the community and has established, the Tooting Neighbourhood Centre, working closely with the borough of Wandsworth in providing services for both its members and the elderly in the wider community.

Another legacy of Bishop Powell and Bishop Bernard along with Rev Philip Mohabir is the establishment of the African & Caribbean Evangelical Alliance (ACEA), which was formed in 1984 as an umbrella organisation to represent Black Pentecostal churches in the UK. Both Bishop Powell and Bishop Bernard were instrumental in nurturing the growth of this organisation, and today they are fondly remembered for this along with the success of the New Testament Assembly worldwide. Both Bishop Powell and Bernard are 'Patriarchs' within the Black Caribbean church community and are two of the early pioneers who helped to establish Black Pentecostal Worship in Britain. Bishop Powell is succeeded by his son, Rev. Delroy Powell who is now the head of the New Testament Assembly.

WOMEN AND THE CHURCHES

Women played a vital part in the development of West Indian churches in Britain and out of the 1000 passengers on board the *Empire Windrush* in 1948, 257 were women and some even travelled alone to get to Britain. Many came with just their small suitcases containing their meagre possession, and one thing we can be sure of is that they packed a bible with them. There were several stowaways on *Empire Windrush* and one of them was a woman. When she was found out, the passengers organised a whip-round and paid her fare. Most of the women on board were on their way to Britain, recruited to work in the newly established National Health Service. They were following in the footstep of Mary Seacole, the illustrious Jamaican nurse, who a century earlier, had also left Jamaica to nurse the soldiers of the Crimean War.

In July 1948, the National Health Service was established to provide free health care for everyone in Britain regardless of income or personal circumstances. It soon ran into trouble with not enough women available to staff it. The problem was, after the war, the women the government was relying on decided to stay at home and raise their families. With this shortage, the government decided to recruit in the West Indies and advertised in local papers for trainee nurses and domestic workers. West Indian women answered the call and came to Britain. However, when they arrived there are many stories that white nurses didn't want to work with them, and as a consequence, many ended up as ancillary workers or in paid jobs in public transport and in factories.

Apart from the women who came to Britain to work, there were also those who came as wives and fiancées, and like their menfolk, came in search of opportunities and to better themselves. Once in Britain, these women combined work with having a family, and they set up businesses, especially in hairdressing and dressmaking, and established community initiatives to make their lives and that of their family more comfortable.

In the churches, women played an important part too. Mother McClaken, for example, started the first Black Pentecostal church in Britain, and throughout the years, women have always been, and still are, the mainstay and backbone of the Black Caribbean church. During the early years, women worked in growing many of the churches and it wasn't unusual for them to play a significant part in raising funds, whether it was for the purchase of a church building or general funds. They ran *pardners,* went out into the community to solicit contributions, baked and sold patties to raise funds, made and secure monetary pledges, and if they had a property of their own, they'd take out a loan on it and give it/lend it to the church. Tithing wasn't generally accepted in Black Pentecostal churches as it is today, and it was very controversial, which meant that churches couldn't rely on it as a source of income.

Unfortunately, women's role in the church was and is still limited. For example, many churches, my father included, had no problem in ordaining women to the ministry and even appointed them to the church board. But women weren't and still are not generally allowed to serve communion, baptise, Bless Babies (Christen), perform marriages, perform burial rights or give, *'the right hand of fellowship,'* which is the way a person is inducted and become a member of a Caribbean Pentecostal church. Women certainly couldn't become a bishop, a point of dispute between my father and one of my aunts who was appointed such. My father refused to recognise her appointment, but they however remained friends throughout their lives, although they disagreed fundamentally on this theological issue.

BISHOP WALTERS-CITY MISSION

One of the women who stood out for me during this period and one I can never forget, is Bishop Walters. She was a remarkable woman in the sea of men and a recognisable presence. I remember my first encounter with her was when she and her group from, *The City Mission Church* came to my father's convention. Although large women and dressed in military uniform, they seem to float in like butterflies. They stood out, looked tall and caused a mild stir as they entered the church. As ministers, they were ushered to the front to sit in the seats reserved for them. I'd seen white Salvation Army women in uniform before but not a Black Pentecostal one dressed as Bishop Walters and her ladies.

Bishop Walters was a 'big' woman with an incredible aura and an all-embracing presence, and I was the one playing the electric organ when they came into the church. They sat down and joined in the service and as soon as a chorus was *raised*, Bishop Walters and her lady friends swung into action. They clapped their hands and exaggeratedly stomped their feet and moaned and groaned as Jazz musicians do when they hit an unusual note or strike a new chord. Walters continued with this throughout the service and during my father's sermon. I was captivated, enthralled as I'd never seen or experienced anything like this before.

I know we clap our hands and stamp our feet but not how Bishop Walters and her ladies did. As the service progressed, I looked forward to when she was *'called'* to speak and all I can remember is that she *'turned the church over!'* What I didn't know then, was that it was 'The City Mission Church in Jamaica, which Bishop Walters belonged to, which pioneered handclapping, and feet-stomping in Pentecostal churches, and here it was, in its purest form, -the real thing-, on display, right before my eyes, and as a young person, I was captivated.

PASTOR I O SMITH

Pastor I O Smith was a different woman to Bishop Walters but no less formidable. Sister Smith as I affectionately remember her, was one of the few women in the early days in West Indian churches, who were not prepared to play a peripheral role or let any male church leader dictate to her and try to keep her in her place. Her vision and calling were far too wide-ranging for that, and she was far too wise to let that get in her way. Despite everything, pastor Smith was a Jamaican woman, and she had the sense of knowing when to strike and when to hold back to fight another day. She knew the barriers she was facing as a Black woman within the church and in society at large. Her pragmatic approach, endeared her to many of the church leaders, and as her brother, Bishop Melvin Powell, founder of the New Testament Assembly, (NTA) was well-liked and respected, and fully supported her, this gave her the courage to pursue her objectives.

Apart from Pastoring an NTA church in Leytonstone, I O Smith set up several community initiatives. These included Youth projects, Christian Training Institutes, a senior citizen club, summer schools and a youth hostel. She was the first Black woman within the Pentecostal church community to actively and consistently work within society, and saw the historic mission of the church as one not confined to the four walls but should be out in *'the byways and hedges'*. Pastor Smith was liked and respected by the British church establishment on account of the work she did in the community. She was the first Black Pentecostal church leader I can remember to be invited to take part in the annual 'Remembrance Day Service' which is held every November at the Cenotaph in London in the presence of the Queen.

In 1994 pastor Smith was awarded an MBE for her community work. She died in Jamaica in 2008 and was a most remarkable, fearless, courageous, and dynamic woman. She had a deep sense of community and is a great example to every Black woman on what can be achieved with effort, determination, and an ability to push through despite the odds.

MUSIC AND THE CHURCH

To understand the Black Pentecostal Church in Britain, it's not only important to understand the faith, it's also important to understand the music and the role it plays, as both are inextricably linked. In its earliest form, West Indian church music in Britain was a mixture of West Indian folk, Anglican hymns, Southern American church songs and revivalist choruses. At first in their services, West Indians hardly had any musical instruments to accompany their singing, -perhaps only a tambourine-, but they would clap their hands and stomp their feet as they sang their hymns and choruses. Within a few years' churches began to attract musicians and it wasn't long before they had at least a guitarist or a person who played the piano. Putting a beat to a hymn or chorus is standard practice in West Indian churches, as is the idea of singing in 'harmony,' which is when a person sings in their own singing voice, *(finding their harmony)* whether it's soprano, alto, tenor or bass.

Most churches had an *adult choir,* but they were not central to the worship. The choir was mainly made up of women and a few men. The women were recognisable in their wide-brim hats, white blouse and black dresses, and the men wore white shirts a tie and black or dark suits. The young people played little part in the life of the church or in the music as they were more 'seen and not heard', and if they were asked to do anything, it was usually to sing, recite a poem, or in my case, 'play a number' on the piano. The prevailing Jamaican music was *Bluebeat,* but this wasn't allowed in the church because it was thought to be ungodly, or what Black Americans call 'devil music'. Jamaicans in the churches even had a word for *Bluebeat,* or unchristian music, they called it 'rags!'

Most musicians in the churches didn't read music either and played their instruments by 'air' or as how they heard the music. This meant that almost anyone who was a musician whether visiting a church or as a member, could play their instrument in any of the services. All they had to do was, set themselves up alongside the existing musicians, and join in and play. At first, this ad hoc arrangement and the range of musical abilities worked reasonably well as most players could be relied on to keep a steady beat, but at times the music was a cacophony of sound, especially when it was amplified. Naturally, there were those with flair and ability, and they stood out, but the music remained largely the same, until the mid 60s when it came under the influence of the songs of the Billy Graham's Crusade. Which is what I'll turn to next.

BILLY GRAHAM CRUSADES AND WEST INDIAN CHURCH MUSIC

In 1954, Billy Graham came to Haringey in North London for a series of evangelistic *'Crusade'* (church services). The *Crusade* was organised by the Evangelical Alliance, and although there was a fuss in the press and in some quarters as to why Billy Graham came, in his first sermon, he explained why.

"We've not come here to the city of London to save England. We have not come here with any great ideas that we are going

to tell you how to do it. We haven't come here to try to reform you. We have come here at the invitation of these churches to help lead you in a Crusade to win men to Jesus Christ and help promote the kingdom of God in Britain." [21]

The original idea was for Billy Graham to stay for one week but the demand to hear him speak was so great, that he ended up staying for three months! From the 1st of March to the 1st of June, Billy Graham filled the 12,000 seater Harringay Arena every night, and even on the last day, the demand was so great to hear him, that the organisers decided to move the final service to the 120,000 seater Wembley stadium. And even that wasn't enough, for all the seats went quickly and there were still thousands who wanted to hear him. The organisers swiftly arranged another service in the afternoon, this time at the White City Stadium in West London to accommodate the extra 65,000 people, who couldn't get into Wembley Stadium!

The Haringey Crusade was a great success, and the number of people who attended is staggering. Over two million people went, with over 40,000 committing their lives to Christ. [22] Although small in numbers, a few West Indians went to Haringey including both my parents. A year later Billy Graham came again to London for a week-long Crusade. It rained every night except for the final night which also turned out to be the coldest night of the year, but this didn't stop 450,000 people turning up during the week to hear him, and 24,000 making a commitment to Christ. [23]

Apart from the numbers, both London Crusades attracted a great deal of publicity and caused a great amount of controversy. The fuss began in the press in 1954 and continued in 1955 until in 1966 it had grown into a full-scale row.

What the fuss was all about, was that the press argued that the reason why so many people went forward to 'accept Christ' at Billy Graham's Crusades, was because of the emotional intensity of his signature song, *Just As I Am*, which the choir always sang before his appeal.

"Just as I am without one plea, but that thy blood was shed for me, and that thou biddest me come to thee, O Lamb of God, I come,"

This song written by Charlotte Elliott *(1789-1871)* an invalid clergyman's daughter, was a favourite of Billy Graham, and was the one song sang at all his Crusades. Charlotte was inspired to write the song after a friend of her father, challenged her in today's language, as to why she hadn't come to faith. Charlotte said that she didn't know how to do so, and the friend told her to *'come to Him just as you are,'* and this is what inspired her to write the song.

In 1966 Billy Graham came again to London but this time to Earls Court for another Crusade. The criticism that began in the press about *'Just as I am'* reached fever pitch, and because of this, Billy Graham decided to drop the song altogether. The irony is that as he made his appeal, but this time in total silence, more people than ever went forward to accept Christ. Cliff Barrows - Billy Graham's musical Director - summed up the reaction this caused.

"We went thirty nights without a single note of the hymn, 'Just as I Am,' has been the signature tune of our Crusades through the years. We had never done that before. When the reporters began to write about the invitation at Earl's Court, they said all

they heard was a shuffling of feet on the floor. 'Bring back 'Just as I Am'! The, silence is killing us!", they wrote." [24]

Apart from the *Just as I Am* controversy, the Earl's Court Crusade was national news for another reason. Cliff Richard, who was then a massive pop star, previously announced that he was a born-again Christian and would be at the Crusade. The press flocked to Earl's Court to cover the story. To put this into perspective, it's like today, Justin Bieber announcing that he is a *born-again Christian* and would be at a church service at the 02 Arena in Central London. In the 1960s, Cliff Richard was a huge star and becoming a *born-again Christian* was big news.

I remember it well as I went with my father to Earl's Court, and after being introduced, Cliff Richards, wearing black rimmed glasses, acoustic guitar in tow, came on to the big stage at Earl's Court. At first, there was this uncanny silence as neither the press nor the 27,000 people present knew what to expect. Cliff confirmed in a few words he was *'a born-again Christian'* and proceeded to sing the well-known Evangelical song, *It's no secret what God can do.* When he finished there was a dignified uproar, and he went outside and repeated this for the thousands of fans who couldn't get into Earl's Court. The following day, this was headline news in all the newspapers.

Although still a relatively small community but substantially more than in 1954, many West Indians went to Earl's Court. They enjoyed this national public display of Evangelical Christianity and returned to their churches spiritually, refreshed and uplifted. Crucially, they took away with them the free songbook with all the songs from the Crusade, and soon they were singing many of them in their services. These included, *Blessed Assurance, The Old Rugged Cross, I Am Thine Oh Lord, Love Lifted Me and How Great Thou Art.* All these songs and others became part of West Indian church music and have remained so ever since.

Fast forward thirty years later and I am at the BBC as a producer on *Songs of Praise* making a programme to commemorate the Anniversary of Billy Graham visit to London. We were able to get Cliff Richards as our special guest, and during the filming, I remember Earls Court and asked, if he would sing again, *It's no secret what God can do.* Editing the programme, I cut from this to the black and white footage of him on stage singing the same number in the same key! This was a magical moment, and I've always wondered whether it was this which won me the Christian Broadcasting Council, Gold Award for Television.

JIM REEVES was another person who significantly influenced West Indian church music. He was a White American international country singer who sang both secular and religious songs. Jim Reeves had many pop hits in the 1950s and 60s, but it was his spiritual/gospel songs that attracted West Indians- religious or not- to his music. Every West Indian home in Britain in the 60s and 70s had a Jim Reeves record, and even those who didn't go to church would always play his music on Sundays. This is how extraordinary influential he was in West Indian circles.

'We Thank Thee' is perhaps Jim Reeve's best-loved gospel album and of the 12 tracks, half, *Never Grow Old, I'll Fly Away, I'd Rather Have Jesus Than Silver or Gold, Across the Bridge, Have Thine Own Way Lord, Where Do I Go From Here and This World is Not My Home,* were all sang regularly in West Indian churches.

West Indians warmed to Jim Reeves' smooth, gentle, baritone voice and his song, *Where Do I Go From Here,* seemed to sum up what many of them felt when in the early days things were hard and they didn't know what the future held. What they knew was that they could always take comfort in the words of his song, *'Where Do I Go from Here'.*

"...lead me through the darkness and through each gloomy day. Take my hand, oh, precious Lord and help me on my way. Give me strength that I might find, abiding faith and peace of mine, and I won't ask, where do I go from here?" [25]

TENNESSEE ERNIE FORD, like Jim Reeves, was another American gospel singer who had an enormous influence on West Indian Church music, and whose songs were commonplace in West Indian Churches. Tennessee was a recording artist in the 1960s/70s who sang Country and 'Southern Gospel' songs. Unlike Jim Reeves, who had a soothing baritone voice, Tennessee's voice although a baritone was more direct, and unlike Jim Reeves, whose gospel was slow and 'country', Tennessee songs appealed to West Indians because they were cheerful and had a mid-tempo beat which suited West Indian church style of singing. Furthermore, many of Tennessee songs could be turned in to choruses which is the highest accolade any song can have in a West Indian Church. Among the popular ones are:

When God Dips His Pen of Love in My Heart, I Can Tell You the Time, I Can Take You to the Place, Have a Little Talk with Jesus, Each Day I'll Do a Golden Deed, On the Jericho Road and Precious Memories. [26]

SOUND OF THE SIXTIES

In the 1960s, young people were some way off from influencing the music of West Indian churches, as that was to come later when several groups emerged with a new sound that were to lay the foundation of what today we know as British gospel music. First among these were the *Soul Seekers,* a group of young men from Camberwell South London who came to Britain with their parents in the 1960s. Other groups like, *'The Singing Stewarts,' 'The Harmonisers', 'The Heavenly Persuaders' and 'The Overcomers'* were equally important.

I must have been around fifteen when the *Soul Seekers* came to my father's church and saw me playing. They asked if I could join them as they were making a change to their line-up and wanted to include a keyboard player. I can't remember what made my father agree to me joining a music group, knowing his views on education, but I'm sure it was my mother who persuaded him, and as a result, I joined the group while still at school, although the rest were full time. The *Soul Seekers* were in their second reincarnation, with a new line-up, Denver and Carl Grant, Ray Powell, John Dyer, Rudolph Richards, and now me.

Denver, the lead guitarist, was a Hank Marvin *(of Cliff Richard & the Shadows)* fan. He was joined by another remarkable musician, his brother-in-law, Ray Powell, who was a Bob

Dylan and Jimi Hendrix enthusiast. What Denver and Ray did was to fuse their musical influences with their West Indian church upbringing to produce a sweet, soulful, country-ish sound, which was accessible and pleasing to a West Indian Christian ear. They both knew that if the music was anything like the prevailing sound of the time, it would be rejected out of hand, but because the music remained within 'accepted limits' and was both modern and relevant, it was accepted. Importantly, it appealed to young people in the churches, who loved and supported it.

What was important about the *Soul Seekers* music was that it was a complete break from the music played in West Indian churches. Here was a group, not a band of musicians, they were self-contained - perhaps the first West Indian church group to do so. They had a new sound, they bought their instruments and amplifiers, bought me an electric organ, and funded their music. Every day they rehearsed in the basement of Denver and Carl's parent's house in Camberwell South London, and I would join them sometimes in the week after school, and at weekends. As a group, they were very professional, even revolutionary for the time, and treated their music in much the same way.

As a group, the *Soul Seekers* was very popular, and were regularly invited to play at church services, programmes, conventions and Church Rallies. Every West Indian church wanted the *Soul Seekers* to come to them, and their fame spread as far as into Europe where they joined the late Rev. Ken McCarthy, (Britain's first gospel promoter), playing to large evangelistic audiences in Holland, Germany, Norway and Sweden where they were well known and usually made the local news whenever they played there. The group signed to Philips Record in Holland and made three records, with *Across the Bridge/Where Shall I Go,* perhaps their best-known number. Some twenty years after the group disbanded, Mike Rimmer reviewing the *Soul Seekers* music in 'Cross Rhythm', described *Across the Bridge/Where Shall I Go,* as:

'A gospel number given a slightly shadows guitar feel,......a blend of pop-gospel and 60s beat music....with great vocals by Tony Massop.'

This is the same Tony Massop who left the group in 1969 and under his new name, Tony Tribe, made the first reggae recording of *Red, Red Wine,* which became a hit, and influenced UB40's, own massive hit of the same song.

THE SINGING STEWARTS

The Singing Stewarts were another pioneering group on the West Indian church scene in the 1960s. They were an a cappella group from Trinidad, who sang *'Spirituals'* and settled in the Midland area of Britain. They consisted of five brothers and three sisters, and as well as being active in the Seventh Day Adventist Church, they also sang at cultural events, hospitals, youth and folk clubs, as well as schools. White audiences warmed to *'The Singing Stewarts easy style* of music and their melodic harmonies.

In 1969 with the release of Edwin Hawkins', *'Oh Happy Day'* and its phenomenal success, PYE records approached the group to do their own version of the same song. Not surprisingly, it didn't do well given the huge success of Edwin's own version, but a chance appearance on a local BBC television programme, *'The Colony',* brought *The Singing*

Stewarts music to the attention of a wider public. On account of this, they received many invitations to perform in Britain and made many appearances in Europe and in America. Later, they were invited to perform at the Edinburgh Festival in Scotland, and this bought their music to an even wider and diverse audience.

'*The Singing Stewarts*' went on to record for a couple of other independent labels, with *Here is a Song* - a mixture of spirituals, by far their most successful. However, by the mid-70s, their style of singing was on its way out being replaced by a new sound (gospel), coming in from America. Eventually, the group disbanded, and Frank Stewart, the mainstay and inspiration, left to seek out other opportunities. After a series of false starts, Frank emerged with a radio show on BBC WM, *The Frank Stewart Gospel Hour,* which ran for over eleven years and became the longest gospel show on British Radio.

In 2012 Frank died, and today he and '*The Singing Stewarts*' are remembered as one of the early pioneers of British gospel music, and Frank is the person who almost single-handedly, created the opening and opportunities, to hear gospel music on BBC radio.

THE HARMONISERS

The Harmonisers were another of the early West Indian church groups in the 1960s who were well known in West Indian church circles. The group was started by, Brother La Touche, who himself was a well-known banjo player and musician, and included, Icilda Cameron, Sam Grizzle, brothers Crossdale and Winston Cumberbatch along with Rudolph Cameron and Carmel Jones. Carmel Jones later went on to set up the Pentecostal Credit Union which in 2020 celebrates its 40th Anniversary.

Like most church groups in the 60s, the Harmonisers played mainly to West Indian church congregations, including rallies and conventions. They made a couple of records for small independent labels who pressed enough copies for them to take round, but not as a commercial endeavour, as the West Indian church market was as yet not 'developed' nor was the church concert scene.

In the 1960s for example, music events like concerts didn't exist in the sense in which we know them today. Virtually all Christian music events were church-based, and as Christian record companies were in their infancy, they too didn't have any real influence on the music. Groups didn't do 'sets' either- or had 'sound checks' or anything like that. What would happen if a group was invited to play at a church, and it would invariably be a service, they would turn up with their instruments and amplifiers, set themselves up alongside the existing musicians and join in and play as part of the musicians for the service. When it was their turn, the group would stand up where they were, the lead singer would walk to the front, and they would play their number - perhaps two or three songs. Once they had finished, they would be expected to join in and play with the rest of the musicians to the end of the service.

THE HEAVENLY PERSUADERS

In the 1960s, music in West Indian churches was happening everywhere and although at first groups tended to stay within their church denomination and locality, they would occasionally make trips to London because that's where the majority of West Indians were, and most churches were located there also. If for example, a group was visiting from outside London, they were likely to meet the *'Heavenly Persuaders'* who were a family group from East London. The group were, brothers, George, John, Noel and Hezi Dyer, and they were joined by their long-time English family friend, Alan Chadwick. They were perhaps the second most well known West Indian church group in London and the *Soul Seekers* main rival.

As a group, the *'Heavenly Persuaders'* came out of the *'Ministry Restoration Church'* in East London which was started by their mother, Dorothy Dyer. Like most church groups at that time, *'The Heavenly Persuaders'* played mainly in the London area, at church services, rallies and conventions, and occasionally they would make the odd trip outside of London, including a celebrated one to Belgium. As a group, they had a distinct sound and style which was controversial. They played reggae which the church disapproved off, but George the elder brother remained firm in his belief that reggae as part of West Indian culture, should be embraced and celebrated. Naturally, in many quarters this went down like a 'ton of bricks', but George continued to steer the group in the musical direction he'd set for it, despite the many criticisms he faced. The point here is that West Indian churches until recently, looked at

Reggae music as being sinful or what Americans call, 'devil music' and would have no association with it.

In the mid 60s, John, the second eldest brother and bass player in the Heavenly Persuaders, left to join the *Soul Seekers.* This was about the same time that I too joined the group, and because we were the 'two outsiders,' (the rest members of the same family), we developed a bond between us which has remained to this day. Eventually, the *'Heavenly Persuaders'* disbanded, and George went on to become a remarkably successful and well-known businessman in the East end of London. In later years, he also became a gospel promoter and staged many landmark reggae gospel concerts, including ones featuring, *Papa San, Carleen Davis and Stichie.* He was also responsible for the success of *Raymond & Co,* the gospel group in the 1990s which his son Raymond fronted.

In 2015 George died and today he is forever remembered, for his pioneering work with the *Heavenly Persuaders,'* his work with *Raymond & Co,* and the contribution he made in making reggae gospel acceptable to a Black Christian church audience. John Dyer, who left the group to join the *Soul Seekers,* is now living in Germany and is still playing, while Noel, one of the other brothers, is today the senior pastor of the family church in Walthamstow, East London.

THE OVERCOMERS

The *Overcomers* was another of the West Indian church groups whose music was influential and controversial during the 1960s. The group was led by Victor Brown a youth leader in the Church of God in Christ, and today the father of Nicky Brown! The line-up consisted of Victor (lead vocalist), Freddie Bradshaw, (bass) Steadman Graham, (organ) Errol Mead, (guitar) and three female vocalists, Audrey and Gloria Bradshaw, and Shelia Edwards. As for the *Overcomers* music, it was outward-looking, and as a group they were not afraid to experiment with well known secular songs as part of their repertoire. This included Jimmy Cliff's, *'Many Rivers to Cross,'* which became a favourite.

In line with Victor's view on where the group should be going, he engaged the services of an agent Jim Merry who agreed to help him get *The Overcomers* into clubs, colleges, universities, and onto the American base in Europe. Victor also asked Merry to help publicise the *Overcomers* recording, *'Stop and Let Me tell You,'* which he wanted to take into clubs and secular venues. This didn't go down too well with the leaders of the church, and Victor was hauled up before them to explain. The problem was that they didn't take kindly to him taking their young people into secular venues and clubs. What they believed, was that Victor was *'bringing disgrace on the church,'* as one of the elders put it.

After struggling with this for a while, Victor decided after a tour of Germany, to disband the group and was forced to give up. Looking back, he believes the tour was a mistake, but because the group had made a democratic decision to tour, he went along with it. The problem was, the *Overcomers* had a record out at the same time, and Victor believe they should have remained in Britain to promote it but chose instead to go to Germany. Victor believes this affected the group's standing with the public, and consequently led to the failure of the record and ultimately his decision to quit. However, what the *Overcomers* had showed and which were to have implications in years to come, was that West Indian church music had a much wider appeal than the church leaders realised.

AMERCIA- THE MOTHER COUNTRY

'Cassocks, Crosses, and Chains'

By the end of the 1960s and the beginning of the 1970s, the West Indian community in Britain felt settled and confident enough to turn their attention to their *'mother'* church in America. Before long they were making regular trips to the United States, taking their young people with them to Conventions and National Assembly Meetings. Laker Airways -the first budget airline in Britain- helped in this process by providing low-cost air fares between London and New York. For many young people, America was both exciting and life-transforming. Young West Indians were impressed with America, especially Black America. In America, Black people seemed far more advanced than in Britain. They held important jobs, were respected members of their communities, owned businesses, were recognised academics, head publications, were on television, in films and were successful artists. They were also in States and National Government, and in America too, Black churches owned their buildings, and the history of their churches, stretched far back into time. They also had modern places of worship, fantastic choirs, wonderful music and their worship was excellent, much freer than in Britain.

Also, Black Americans didn't seem so hung up on rules and regulations as the churches were in Britain, and furthermore, nothing like this existed back home. All in all, America was a real eye-opener!

Many of these visits were also made at the time when the *Civil Rights Movement* was still being played out in America and although Martin Luther King had died a few years earlier in 1968, his influence was still everywhere, especially in Black Americans churches and in their communities. To these young West Indians who made these trips, here was a Black churchman they felt they knew, for he preached in a style and manner they were accustomed to. Moreover, they felt they could learn from him how to bring about change in their own lives and in society. This was powerful and inspiring, and King's message found fertile ground in the minds of these young people.

Apart from the backdrop of the *Civil Rights Movement,* these trips were also made at a time when in America, themes like *'Black is Beautiful,' 'Black Pride'* and *'Say it Loud, I'm Black and I'm Proud'* were potent symbols of Black Identity, *'Black Hope',* and *'Black Aspiration.'* This too had an enormous impact on the young people, and they began to look at themselves and their church in a new and 'conscious' way.

West Indian pastors too were changed by these trips, and as soon as they got back to Britain, many began to make changes in their churches and implement some of the things they had seen in America. For example, some pastors began to restructure their church along American lines, and terms like 'Diocese' 'Prelate' and 'First Lady,' entered Caribbean church lexicon for the first time. Others started to wear clerical gowns and collars which was something unheard off before these visits, and a few pastors even started to wear cassocks, crosses, and chains, again something inconceivable, before America.

Although these visits to The United States were exciting, eye-opening, and life-changing, they weren't without controversy. One of the first things that surprised many young people was that although the leadership in their churches in Britain was Black, in America in the *'mother church,'* the reverse was true, with an almost exclusive white leadership and congregation. As a 'mother church' based in the American South, nobody had told them what this meant politically and socially. However, not quite gotten over this shock, they were soon faced with another surprise. This time, they couldn't believe what they were seeing in the National Assembly, Christian women wearing, jewellery and make-up, and the Black women straightened their hair!

All this was routinely banned and condemned in the church back in Britain as 'sinful and ungodly', and here in the 'mother church', they were openly on display. The contradiction was clear, but what was interesting, is that although these women wore makeup and jewellery, they were no less spiritual, nor did what they wore seems to inhibit the flow of the Holy Spirit. This was deeply influential, and as soon as the young people got back to Britain, they began to challenge many of the inherent contradictions they now saw in their churches.

America had opened their eyes as to what was possible and permissible in the 'mother church' but not allowed in their own church in Britain. Young people especially the women argued for change, but many pastors resisted, and rather than sanctioning a relaxation of the rules to fall in line with the 'mother church,' or negotiate an agreed compromise, stood firm and held on to an untenable position. The result was that many young people left the church as it seemed to be stuck in 'the dark ages.'

In all fairness, what the pastors were doing was holding on to what they knew and what they themselves had been brought up to believe. But because they were unwilling or unable to change, they helped to precipitate and hasten the exodus of many young women and men from the church. The beneficiaries were the independent churches that began to spring up all over London and in many of the big cities. However, those women who remained, simply ignored the teaching on jewellery and make-up, and soon it didn't matter anymore, for as Black Independent Christian women, they weren't going to be defined by what they wore, but by who they were as Christians.

Despite all this, many lives were changed by these visits to America and many young people came back to Britain determined to bring about change in their own lives and the life of their church. Many of today's Black Pentecostal leaders are the product of this experience, and many of the leading figures in British gospel music, attribute the spark that lit their initial interest, to these early visits to America.

THE SPIRITUALS

Many of the young people who made the trips to the United States were musicians or aspiring artists, and the gospel music they heard there, has its origins in the *'Spirituals.'* This is the music that originated in the Southern States of America and developed against the background of the Atlantic slave trade, -the period from the 16-19th century when millions of Black people were forcibly taken from Africa and transported to America and the West Indies to work on plantations. Once in the *'new world'*, slaves worked in producing the cash crops, -cotton, sugar, tobacco, coffee etc, - that made Britain and America, the economic powerhouse they became. On the plantations, slaves worked from dawn to dusk, and endured unbelievable hardship and brutality. Only the fittest and strongest slaves survived, and Mary Prince, a former slave, in 1831 published an account of what it was like to be a slave.

"I have often wondered how English people can go out into the West Indies and act in such a beastly manner... when they go to the West Indies, they forget God and all feelings of shame; I think since they can see and do such things, they tie up people like hogs –moor them up like cattle, and they lick them, so as dogs, or cattle, or horses never were flogged." (The History of Mary Prince - A West Indian Slave, 1831)

This type of brutality was typical, and to ease the suffering and cruelty of their daily lives, slaves would sing. They sang as they worked, planted, picked the crops and later when they worked on the railroads. Whenever and wherever slaves found themselves, they sang. These *'work songs'* as they became known, drew their inspiration from the Bible, especially the Old Testament, and tells of a time 'when God's people in bondage, was set free.' Slaves would sing their *songs* both to ease their burden and to fill their hearts with the hope of a day when they too would be free. Slave owners encouraged slaves to sing, because they realised the more, they sang, the better they worked, and the more productive they became.

For the plantation system to work smoothly and efficiently, slaves were forced to be obedient, submissive, and above all prevented from escaping. We don't hear too much about slave rebellion and resistance, but there were many, and slaves were forever resisting and whenever they could, they would escape and run away. To prevent this, slave masters were particularly brutal, and to reinforce the subjugation of their slaves, they compelled them to attend their church, and there at the back or in the gallery, away from the white congregation, they would sit in silence, and hear the hymns of British hymn-writers, Isaac Watts and Charles Wesley. They could easily identify with many of these, especially those that described the suffering of Christ, for example, *When I survey the wondrous cross* or *Oh God our help in ages past*, a condition not too dissimilar to their own.

Apart from the hymns, slaves also heard in their master's church that it was their duty to follow their master's instructions, as it was the 'way of the Lord.'

"Servants, obey in all things your master according to the flesh, not with eye service, as men-pleasers; but in singleness of heart, fearing God". Colossians 3 v 22

Slave masters often quoted this when administering punishment, cynically believing that this would make the slaves accept their lot and deter them from rebelling and running away.

Slaves too ironically kept their own 'church', and although they were not allowed to assemble as a group, they would often meet in secret, usually at some distance from the master's house. Here at these *'campground meetings',* they would fuse the hymns they'd heard in church, with the music they'd kept from Africa, and create a sound that laid the foundation of what today we call the *'Spirituals,'* - the precursor of gospel music.

Both Watts and Wesley were radical hymn writers who broke prevailing conventions. Watts, for example, wrote hymns taken from the Psalms, but not quoted directly from it, which was the prevailing orthodoxy of the time. Wesley was a clergyman who travelled around England on horseback preaching the gospel rather than doing so in church, and his brother Charles wrote the hymns to accompany his preaching. The method they both used in their personal life and their approach to holiness, earned them the nickname-Methodist, because of the methodical way they approached their faith. The Methodist Church denomination was established by their followers after their deaths.

Slaves were forever plotting to escape and they used *'work songs'* to communicate their plans and to conceal them from their masters. In the West Indies, slaves too used *'work songs'* similarly and used them to communicate among themselves, and to mock their masters, who were largely unaware of their meaning. In America, Christian slaves are thought to be the first to introduce these songs as coded messages, and in the West Indies, some of them seem to have come down to us through the ages as choruses, possibly echoing coded information of a time long past. Here are some well known examples.

"Meet Me by the River, someday, meet me by the river not far away, when my work on earth is done and my Lord shall call me home, happy, happy home, beyond the sky, meet me by the river, someday."

"It Soon Be Done all my troubles and trials when we get home on the other side. I'm going to shake my hands with the elders, tell all my people 'good morning,' I'm going to sit down beside my Jesus; I'm going to sit down and rest a little while."

In America, *The Gospel Train* (is coming), *Steal Away, Swing Low, Sweet Chariot* and *Go Down Moses* are some of the best-known Spirituals that contains coded messages of escape plans. The message in *Go Down Moses* is that an escape is imminent, in *The Gospel Train* (is coming), is that the way is clear to escape, and *Steal Away* operated on two levels. The first that the escape planned could go-ahead (Steal Away) and on the second level, that if a slave couldn't be free in this life, then they would prefer to *'steal away to Jesus,'* in other words, they'd rather die.

In Britain today, *Swing Low, Sweet Chariot* is perhaps the best known of all the *Spirituals*, mainly because fans sing it at English International Rugby matches. The composer is unknown, but the song is thought to have been written around 1865 by a former slave, Wallis Willis, and became famous in

1906 when the Fisk Jubilee Singers made a recording of it. The coded message in *Swing Low, Sweet Chariot* is that it told slaves who had decided to escape, what to do and where to run. Below is the song with its hidden, coded message.

SWING LOW, SWEET CHARIOT [27]

Words	Meanings	Coded Messages
Swing low:	*Come down here low:*	*There is a safe house*
Sweet chariot:	*Chariot from Heaven:*	*The 'Underground Railroad' (safe houses)*
Coming for to carry me home:	*Take me to heaven:*	*Freedom*
I looked over Jordan And what did I see:	*I looked in the Bible:*	*The Mississippi River*
A band of angels:	*Angels coming:*	*People on the Underground Railroad who helped slaves to escape.*
Coming after me:	*Die and go to heaven:*	*Escape to the North or Canada.*

FISK JUBILEE SINGERS

The Fisk Jubilee Singers were the first real exponents of *The Spirituals* or 'slave work songs,' who at the turn of the century made their appearance in exceptional circumstances. They were a group of Black singers from Nashville Tennessee who were among the first students of Fisk Free Coloured School, formed in 1866 by the American Missionary Association, to provide 'a liberal education for young men and women irrespective of colour' - in other words, slaves. In 1871, the school found itself in severe financial difficulties and faced with the risk of closing, its treasurer and music director, George Leonard White, decided to form a group of singers, (four Black men and five Black women), and take them on the road to raise $20,000 to save the school. White named the group after Fisk, but more importantly, he included in the name the word 'Jubilee', *(yobel)* which is a time in the Old Testament when anyone who owed a debt, was set free to make a new start, and a time when the children of Israel committed themselves to liberty and freedom from tyranny.

And ye shall hallow the fifth year and proclaim liberty throughout all the land unto all the inhabitants thereof: It shall be a jubilee unto you, and ye shall return every man unto his possession, and ye shall return every man unto his family........Ye shall not, therefore, oppress one another, but thou shall fear the Lord God: For I am the Lord your God.'
-Leviticus 25: 10-17

This was fitting because Leviticus was the book in the bible that slave owners often quoted to justify slavery, and the one they used when meting out punishment to their slaves.

At first, the tour didn't go well as white audiences reacted adversely to the anthems, sentimental songs and ballads the singers performed. They also didn't like the group singing in a European style, for they believed they were getting 'above themselves,' nor did they take kindly either to the singers wearing fine clothes and singing, 'like white people'. It was only when the group started to sing *'spirituals', 'slave work songs,'* that white American audiences began to warm to them, and things began to change. White Americans seemed to enjoy the *spirituals*, they liked the work songs, and as the singers were able to sell their sheet music during the intermissions, this helped to publicise the tour and helped to spread their fame across America. Soon they were receiving invitations to perform, including one from President Ulysses Grant in 1872, who invited them to the White House.

As the Jubilee tour continued, it was clear that their performances were influencing white America. For the first time, white Americans were hearing the songs born out of slavery and the plight and suffering of a people they had subjugated for so long. Mark Twain, (1835-1910) the celebrated American writer who himself was born in the South, and whose father was a slave owner, wrote about the singers.

'It was the first time for twenty-five or thirty years that I had heard such songs, or heard them sung in the genuine old way- and it is away, I think, that white people cannot imitate-and never can for that matter, for one must have been a slave himself in order to feel what that life was, and so convey the pathos of it in the music. [28]

FISK JUBILEE SINGERS IN BRITAIN

In 1873, the Fisk Jubilee Singers came to Britain and performed throughout the country in churches, concert halls, and at private parties for aristocrats, politicians, and leading churchmen. They were feted by the Duke and Duchess of Argyll, introduced to Lord Shaftesbury, and sang for both William Gladstone the British Prime Minister, and for Queen Victoria. The queen was so impressed with them and their performance of *'Steal away',* that she commissioned a painting of them, which today hangs in the Jubilee Hall of their University in Nashville.

Performing for Queen Victoria and members of the British Establishment, opened many doors for the group, and Charles Spurgeon, founder of the Metropolitan Tabernacle at the Elephant and Castle in London and one of the great Victorian Baptist preachers, invited the group to sing at his church. The Metropolitan Tabernacle was the largest Protestant church in London, and when the singers sang there on the 30th of July 1873, more than 6,000 people turned up, with hundreds more turned away. The choir collected £220 – a huge sum- for their university, and Spurgeon is quoted in the South London Press as saying:

Our friends seem to sing from their hearts. They seem to preach in their singing, and this gives a force to the music such as no other thing could. They have touched my heart...This is a real mystery and a deep theology in this singing that we can hardly understand. We have not been placed under the same circumstances. Very few of us have had our backs tingling under the lash and have never had to work on a cotton plantation. [29]

While in Britain, the singers travelled North, doing concerts in Scotland, York, Hull, and Newcastle. In Newcastle, they met the celebrated American Evangelist Dwight L Moody and Ira D Sankey, who were both pioneers of large-scale evangelistic services. They sang at many of their meetings, and whenever they could, the two Evangelists would always ask the group to sing, *'Steal Away to Jesus'* and *'There are Angels hovering round,'* - two of their favourites.

Before returning to America, Fisk toured, continental Europe, and with subsequent tours to Australia, New Zealand, India, Hong Kong, and Japan, they'd raised enough money to pay the debt owed to the school, with enough left over, to fund Fisk, as a fully-fledged university.

GOSPEL GREATS

The Holiness Churches

Between 1863, the *Emancipation Proclamation* and the *13th Amendment* in *1865*, thousands of freed slaves left the American south - the land of slavery and subjugation - to migrate to the north in search of work, freedom, equality and a better way of life. While in the North, their music met a new religion that began in the 'holiness churches' and was finding fertile ground in Black communities. This new religion, Pentecostalism, was different from the religion the ex-slaves knew or were used to. For example, the new religion didn't try to imitate a European style of worship or singing but expressed a freer and more culturally appropriate form. In the 'holiness churches,' people played drums, guitars, banjos and tambourines. They clapped their hands, stomped their feet, shouted, hollered, and sang in a *call and response* manner that every ex-slave knew. Soon the *Spirituals* that the ex-slave had brought with them from the South, began to adapt and change as it met the new religion of the 'holiness churches. It would, however, take the skill and influence of a few people to propel the music forward into the modern age. One of the first to do this was Charles A Tindley, a Methodist minister, singer, writer, and composer.

CHARLES A TINDLEY (1851-1933) was the founder of one of the largest African American churches. He was born in Maryland a slave state, and although his father was a slave, his mother was free. Tindley's mother died when he was four and at the age of five, he was separated from his father. Unable to read and write, Tindley taught himself how to do so, and by the time he was seventeen, he could read and write fluently. Like most Black Americans, his life began to change after the declaration of Emancipation and the ending of the American Civil War. He met and married Daisy Henry, and like many of his contemporaries, migrated North for the chance of a better life. Together they ended up in Philadelphia where Tindley found work as a janitor at the Bainbridge Street Methodist Episcopal church. He worked there in the days, enrolled at night school, took a correspondence course in Hebrew and Greek, and earned a doctorate in the process. In 1885 he was ordained a minister and spent the next seventeen years as an itinerant preacher. In 1902, he was asked to become the minister at Bainbridge Street Church, the same place he worked when he first arrived in Philadelphia.

Tindley was an excellent preacher with a considerable reputation. He was also a great composer of Christian music and wrote hundreds of songs, many of which were influenced by the hymns he knew. His songs were freer and less inhibited than the 'Spirituals,' and he would include musical instruments to accompany them. Tindley often interspersed his preaching with the songs he'd written, and in 1916 published a collection of his songs *in New Songs of Paradise.* Five years later, he had six songs in *'Gospel Pearls',* an anthology of church songs, published mainly for Black American churches.

Today, many of Tindley's songs are considered gospel 'greats' with

'Nothing Between My Soul and the Saviour,' 'By and By When the Morning Come' and *'Leave it There,' (Take Your Burden to the Lord)*, considered among his finest. *'I'll Overcome Someday'* is another of Tindley's song, which many people believed influenced the civil rights anthem, *'We Shall Overcome.'* His other great song *'Stand By Me When the Storms of Life Are Raging,'* is also thought to have inspired Ben E King's, *'Stand By Me,'* which became a big pop hit in the 1960s, and in 2018 was given a new outing by 'The Kingdom Choir' at the Royal Wedding of Prince Harry and Meghan Markle at Windsor Castle in the UK.

Unlike many Christian songwriters, Tindley's lyrics speaks about both body and soul, as he believed a person's material well-being was equally important as their soul. He was able to demonstrate what he meant by this when during the 1920s Great Depression, he turned his church basement into a soup kitchen to help those in need. Tindley cared about people and because of this set up several initiatives to support members of his church and others in the wider community. For example, he established a saving club to help people buy their homes, and took great interest in young people, encouraging them into education. He was also helpful in urging people to start their own businesses, and he actively took a stand on social and political issues when he thought it degraded Black people.

Today, Tindley is recognised as the grandfather of 'gospel music' and one of its greatest exponents. Before he died in 1933, he had established one of the largest African American Methodist church, which started with a congregation of 200 and rose to over 12,000 members by the time he died. As a tribute to him, the Bainbridge Street Methodist Episcopal church where he first worked and made his name, was renamed, Tindley Temple.

THOMAS DORSEY (1899-1993) is the next great influence on the music of the *'Spirituals,'* and it was *Dorsey* it is thought who coined the phrase 'gospel music.' He was born in Georgia, where his father was a Baptist minister and his mother a church pianist. Dorsey learnt to play the piano when he was young and played many of Tindley's songs. In the 1930s, he left Georgia for Chicago, and while there became a blues singer, pianist and composer, playing for Ma Rainey - a famous blues singer. After experiencing a series of personal setbacks, along with harbouring a belief that God was calling him to use his talent in the church, Dorsey turned his back on the blues and began to write and compose 'gospel' songs.' He became a member of the Pilgrim Baptist Church in Chicago and eventually its musical director, a post he held for over 40 years.

Dorsey's style of gospel music combined African American church hymns with blues and jazz influences. This aroused the wrath of the churches in Chicago and they refused to include any of his gospel songs in their services, criticising him for bringing the blues, i.e. 'devil's music' into the church. On many occasions, Dorsey said he was thrown out of 'some of the best churches in Chicago,' but believing this is what God wanted him to do, he continued to compose gospel songs, playing them and selling his sheet music. At first, he found it hard to get his music published by any of the leading publishing houses in Chicago, and as a result, in 1932 set up his own publishing company 'The Dorsey House of Music', becoming the first Black independent publisher of gospel music in America.

In the same year Dorsey wrote his most famous song, '*Take My Hand, Precious Lord,*' which many people know simply as '*Precious Lord.*' '*Precious Lord*' is a song born out of tragedy, pain and loss, and represents a soul so weak, tired and worn, that its only hope is to rely on God to keep it from falling apart. As a song, it was composed after Dorsey while away in St Louis, received news that his wife, Nellie who was in the final month of pregnancy died while giving birth. And if this was not bad enough, although the baby was born safely, it too died a few days later. Stricken with immense grief and pain, Dorsey in his own words said:

"I became very despondent and filled with grief. A few days later I visited my good friend, Professor Frye. We walked around the campus of Annie Malone's Poro College for a while and then went into one of the music rooms. I sat down at a piano and began to improvise on the keyboard. Suddenly, I found myself playing a melody that I hadn't played before. As I played, I started to say, 'Blessed Lord,' 'blessed Lord,' 'blessed Lord.' My friend walked over to me and said, 'Why don't you make that Precious Lord?" [30]

Dorsey said he got a few 'Amen' on that, and the words of '*Precious Lord*' began to formulate in his mind, eventually becoming one of the greatest gospel songs, ever written. In his excellent book, 'An illustrated history of Gospel, Steve Turner sums up the colossal impact Tomas Dorsey has had on gospel music.

What existed before Dorsey were a number of tributaries, often difficult to identify or trace back to a source. What came after him (Dorsey) was a mighty river of gospel music, almost all of it owing something to him. From his coaching, writing, performing, directing, organising, and publishing, gospel music grew to be an industry, that would soon have its own record labels, publishing houses, writers, conventions, touring circuits, stars and legends. Before Dorsey there were, guitar evangelists, singing preachers, Jubilee choirs, harmony quartets and sacred soloists, but after Dorsey, there was only gospel! [31]

Apart from helping to steer gospel music into the modern age, Dorsey is also credited with introducing the world to Mahalia Jackson, the greatest gospel singer ever, and the music's first superstar. He first met Mahalia in Chicago in 1937, and they began to work together, with Dorsey writing gospel songs and Mahalia delivering them in her unique and inimitable style. Together they both helped to propel gospel music into the modern age and set it in a new and exciting direction.

Dorsey's influence on gospel music is colossal. He co-founded, *The National Gospel Choir Convention,* and during the Golden Age of Gospel Music (1940-50), his impact on the music was immense and his influence was everywhere. Almost every gospel artist in America during this time recorded a Dorsey song, and the effect he had could be heard in the music of *The Dixie Hummingbirds, The Soul Stirrers with Sam Cooke, The Sensational Nightingales, The Five Blind Boys of Mississippi,* and in the music of *Sister Rosetta Tharpe* who toured Britain in the 1950s. Dorsey's music also influenced *Clara Ward, Albertina Walker and the Caravans* and much nearer our time, *James Cleveland, Edwin Hawkins, and Andréa Crouch.*

Dorsey wrote hundreds of songs, 200 of which are gospel. His three most famous are, *it's a Highway to Heaven, Peace in the valley and Precious Lord* which was a favourite of Martin Luther King and was sung the night before he was assassinated. Mahalia Jackson sang it at Dorsey's own funeral, and President Lyndon B Johnson requested it at his. Today, Dorsey's archive is appropriately housed at Fisk University in Nashville Tennessee.

MAHALIA JACKSON (1911-1972) is perhaps the best-known gospel singer the world has ever known. She was born in New Orleans, Louisiana on October 26, 1911, and started singing in church when she was only four. Mahalia moved with her parents to Chicago in her teens and became a member of the Greater Salem Baptist Church. Although brought up a devout Christian, Mahalia admired Bessie Smith and Ma Rainey - two giants of the blues - but she never had any inclination herself to sing anything other, than gospel music. In 1937, Mahalia was introduced to Thomas Dorsey, and worked with him for fourteen years, accompanying him to gospel concerts, where she sang his songs, while he sold the sheet music.

An entrepreneur at heart, Mahalia realised that she wasn't going to make a living solely from gospel music and took a beauty course to provide an income for herself. After graduating, she opened a beauty salon in Chicago, working in the week and leaving the weekends to her music. Soon she began to attract a lot of attention with her unique brand of gospel singing, and it was while working with Dorsey in 1937 that she came to the attention of Decca Records who signed her to the label.

Mahalia achieved moderate success with Decca, and it was when she moved to Apollo Records that she had her first big hit, *Move on Up a Little Higher,* which was helped by Stud Terkel, a white DJ who played the song alongside the rhythm and blues records he played on his radio show. The record went on to sell eight million copies and established Mahalia as a top recording artist. Soon, concert tours and appearances came flooding in and Mahalia became so popular that she was given her own radio show. She made a few more recordings with Apollo - the most famous being, *In the Upper Room,* 'which further cemented her reputation.

In 1954, Columbia Record came calling believing they could make her into a top International crossover artist. Mahalia signed to them and became a massive recording star. With increase recording success, she was now much in demand for concert tours, radio, and television appearances. She performed on the Ed Sullivan show, appeared at the Carnegie Hall in New York, and was featured in the film, *Imitation of Life.* She toured Europe, appeared on the BBC, was popular in Norway and France, and made many memorable appearances there. She also appeared at the Newport Jazz festival to great acclaim, and has her fame rose, Mahalia was invited to perform with legendary stars like Louis Armstrong and Duke Ellington.

During her lifetime, Mahalia turned down many offers to sing secular music and even refused to sing songs that were not religious. She wouldn't sing in places considered inappropriate either, or songs that didn't reflect her Christian faith. As a friend of Dr Martin Luther King, Mahalia was active in the Civil Rights Movement and in 1963 sang at the well-known *'March on Washington'* where Martin Luther King made his famous, *'I Have a Dream'* speech. In 1961 she was invited to sing at the Inauguration of President John F Kennedy, and in 1968, sang *Precious Lord* at Dr Martin Luther King's funeral. Ironically when she died in 1972, a young Aretha Franklin sang, *Precious Lord* at her own funeral, as if the baton of gospel music had passed on from one generation to the next.

AFRICANS ARRIVAL IN BRITAIN

From the 1970s onwards, people from the West Indies preferred to be known as Caribbean rather than West Indian, and what most British people knew of them, is what they saw each Sunday, Caribbean Christians making their way to church, their women, dressed in smart colourful clothes, with their men folks and children following alongside. In all fairness, that's about all they knew, and it wasn't surprising, because most Caribbean churches generally kept themselves to themselves and although they were experiencing enormous growth, they largely kept away from mainstream society, concentrating on consolidating their position in Britain. Overall, Caribbean people felt settled in Britian, and as they began to ease themselves into British society, a parallel development was also taking place. Africans had begun to arrive in Britain. In the 1960s they came mainly as students who were sent by their governments to acquire the education and skills needed for development. Those who had children while in Britain took them back to Africa after they graduated, and now in the 1970s and 80s, these same children as adults were back, but this time joined by a new wave of Africans who also came in search of jobs and economic opportunities.

In his excellent book, *Look What The Lord Has Done*, Mark Sturge explains some of the reasons, why Africans came. He says for example, that during the 1970s and 80s, this was a time of political and economic instability and unrest in Africa, and a period of coup d'état and civil wars. This acted as a 'push factor' in propelling Africans to Britain, and with the economic opportunities the country offered, and existing family ties, this pulled Africans in, drawing them into the country. In later years, the 'Celtic Tiger boom' in the Irish Republic, merely added to this, a point I only realised when in 2016 I visited Ireland and was surprised to see so many Africans there.

Historically, Africans, like the Caribbean before, have been in Britain for hundreds of years. One of the first African church in Britain was
'The Sumner Road Chapel', which was started in London in 1906 by a Ghanaian schoolteacher, Rev Thomas Kwame Brem-Wilson. Like West Indians before, Africans, *(Nigerians and Ghanaians),* -the two largest groups-, were surprised at how unchristian Britain was, and how much Christianity was in decline when they too arrived in the 1980s. It didn't take long however, for them to get started and set up their churches, establish their branch of Christianity and set about *re-evangelising* Britain, a task they term, *'reverse mission.'* In other words, in much the same way that Britain once brought Christianity to Africa, Africans now believe that they must help *'turn Britain back to God'.*

WHAT DO WE KNOW ABOUT AFRICAN CHURCHES?

Today Black Africans are most of the Black population in Britain with around 1.2 million people. In London, this is even more pronounced as Black Africans now account for 7% of the population in the capital and Caribbean about 4.2%. The result is that Black Pentecostal church membership has increased dramatically and according to the Evangelical Alliance's Census *'Ethnicity and Regular Church Going',* this growth is reflected in Black church attendance too, which is at least three times their proportion in the population. In London, 48% of all churchgoers are now black and the Borough of Southwark in South East London has the largest concentration of African Churches, with an estimated 240 Black Majority churches with over 20,000 congregants. [32]

This growth in the African church community has had several effects on the overall level of Christianity in Britain. One of the results is that it has helped to boost the overall church attendance in the country, as well as it has increased the demand for gospel music. African churches are now the fastest growing in the UK, and like Caribbean before, Africans have a high incidence of churchgoing which has helped to change the perception that Christianity in Britain is in terminal decline. London is the place where this perception is at its sharpest, and it is in London which has seen the greatest growth. For example, between 2005 and 2012 church attendance in London has grown from just over 620,000 people in 2005 to over 720,000 in 2012, a 16 per cent increase. While this increase is across all denominations, the greatest area of growth is in the so-called, Black majority church, where the African church now dominates.[33] But what do we know about African churches, their Christianity, and their rapid growth? Below are the main African Churches who are leading the way in this new development.

KINGSWAY INTERNATIONAL CHRISTIAN CENTRE (KICC)

KICC is perhaps the most famous of African churches in Britain and since it was formed in 1992, its growth has been spectacular. The church was formed by Nigerian Pastor, Matthew Ashimolowo, and the way he has grown the church is an example worthy of consideration. From the start, Pastor Matthew realised the power of the media and wasn't afraid to use it. He hired Paul Cunningham a Christian PR specialist to help him. Paul once ran a Fleet Street advertising agency and was able to attract mainstream coverage for the church. I remember, how surprised I was when working for the BBC and on my way to Manchester, I picked up a couple of newspapers at Euston station as I regularly do, and was surprised to see KICC splashed over the front pages of the 'Times' and 'The Guardian'. I simply couldn't believe what I was seeing and rang Marcia Dixon, a church PR specialist herself to find out more, and to see who was behind this. Marcia told me about Paul Cunningham and for a short time afterwards, I was able to observe Paul at close quarters, and even worked with him, producing KICC's, promotional video, when Pastor Matthew was thinking of purchasing an area of land in Finsbury Park North London to build his church headquarters.

Along with the mainstream media, Matthew also used the Christian media, especially Premier Radio and God TV to help him grow KICC. Not since the Billy Graham crusades have any independent church in Britain used the Christian media the way Pastor Matthew did and so effectively. Not only did he sponsor Premier radio programmes including Muyiwa's 'Gospel Tonight, but' he also did the same on God

TV and advertise incessantly on both. In the early years, you couldn't turn on Premier Radio and God TV, without hearing information about one of KICC's services.

Pastor Matthew's third move was to create a high-profile event, his flagship conference, *'Gathering of Champions,'* with the strapline, *'Raising champions, taking territories',* which for many years, was the 'must-attend' event and the biggest conference in the Black Pentecostal church in Britain. Thousands of people went each year to *'Gathering of Champions'* to hear the best American and African preachers, and to hear the best gospel artists. Many of the biggest Black American preachers came to *'Gathering of Champions'* and for many years, Eddie Long, TD Jakes, Juanita Bynum, and Donnie McClurkin were frequent visitors. Apart from a few setbacks, KICC remains one of the biggest Black Pentecostal churches in Britain today, with a membership of over 12000. It's now based outside London and operates from its £5 million, 4-acre, multi-site complex, in Chatham, Kent.

THE REDEEMED CHRISTIAN CHURCH OF GOD (RCCG)

This is a Nigerian church, which was started in 1952 and today is led by Pastor Adeboye. It is one of the largest Pentecostal churches in the world, with over 2000 parishes and a worldwide membership of 28 million people represented in over 198 countries. In Nigeria, the church is famous for its 'first Friday of the month' all-night prayer service which regularly attracts over 500,000 people.

The UK branch of the Redeemed Christian Church of God was started in 1988 and today is under the leadership of Pastor

Agu Irukwu, who twenty years ago was sent to Britain from Nigeria to look after the fledging church in London. Today, RCCG is the largest Black Pentecostal church in Britain with around 80,000 members in 8,000 parishes. From its base in Brent Cross West London, the church holds weekly services attended by more than 2000 people. It is a high-profile church and in recent years have received both royal and senior politicians to its services. Each year the church holds a spectacular prayer meeting at the Excel Centre in London where it regularly attracts over 40,000 people. Today, The Redeemed Christian Church of God is spearheading the drive to re-evangelise Britain and have recently teamed up with some of the long-established evangelical churches in Britain, looking at creative ways to do this.

THE DEEPER LIFE CHURCH

The Deeper Life Church is the personal story of Nigerian W.F. Kumuyi, a former Anglican and university lecturer who in 1973, along with 15 students started the church in Nigeria as a bible study group. Today, *Deeper Life* is one of the biggest churches in Nigeria and in 1988 it opened a branch in a community hall at The Elephant and Castle in London pioneered by Pastor Pre Ovia. The church in Britain now has over 65 branches with other *Deeper Life* churches in the Republic of Ireland, Bulgaria, Spain, Germany, Netherlands, Sweden, America, Jamaica and New Zealand.

In his book, *'Deeper Life, The Extraordinary Growth of the Deeper Life Bible Church,'* Alan Isaacson chronicles the growth and development of the church and explains the extraordinary skill of Dr Kumuyi who has grown the church from its small beginnings to what it is today,- a two million international member church. In London, the numbers are not as large, but its size is not insignificant, as in recent years the church has purchased a former cinema in Clapham Junction to hold services for its congregation of over 2000 people.

WHAT DO WE KNOW ABOUT AFRICAN CHURCHES?

8 THINGS TO KNOW

(1) African Christianity is an active one

African Christianity like its early Caribbean counterpart is an active, rather than a passive faith, and African churches expect their members to become involved in the life and activities of the church. It's not just about going to church on a Sunday or a weekday and passively taking part, but getting involved, whether it's being part of a group, meeting and making friends, proclaiming the gospel publicly, volunteering or being part of any of the church activities. It's also about seeing Christianity as an active faith and not one which is about adhering to church, rules, rites, rituals and ceremonies. African Christianity is part of everyday life, every aspect of it and not reduced to a few hours on Sundays, or at special church services or a faith that's only practised privately. *The Eucharist* is not the centre of worship in African churches but a part of it, and as such it's not the focal point of any service or the core part of an individual's faith. African Pentecostals, like Pentecostals generally, emphasise a personal experience and relationship with God, and this involves an active response.

(2) African Churches have a positive outlook on life

African churches in Britain today are probably some of the best equipped Pentecostal churches in the country. Their leaders are generally inspirational, have skill, ability, and expertise. At its head is usually a charismatic leader often with a strong personality. The church demand and get a high level of commitment from its members, who both volunteer their time, and give 10% of their pay to the church as a tithe.

As a church group, their members are aspirational, they have a positive outlook on life and their Christianity sees prosperity as God's blessing, and as a reward for their commitment and sacrifice. There is a lot the established church in Britain can learn from African churches, and many are doing so, putting in strategies to attract more people, including Black members to their services. The whole notion of 'diversity,' in established churches is an example of this, and an indication of new ways of 'doing church' in the modern age which African Christians are good at.

(3) African Churches know how to grow a church in the modern age

African Christians think big and love the term, *'my God is a big God',* which is an indication on the limitless power of what God can do. Many of them started with a few members and in record time have grown into big churches. The Redeemed Christian Church of God is a church that actively and even aggressively pursues, 'church growth.' The church aims to have a Redeem branch 'within ten minutes walking distance,' of anywhere in the country, and it's this strategy which has seen the church grow its parishes within twenty years, from a few members to over 800, and a membership today of over 80,000. Even today when African churches put on events, conferences, special services, music concerts etc, they are likely to be on a grand scale like *Kingsway's 'Gathering of Champions'* or *The Redeemed* prayer meeting which attracts over 40,000 people at the Excel Centre in London.

African churches apply the same positive idea when seeking out a church or somewhere to worship, and are the first to look for warehouses, former bingo halls, shop fronts, abandoned halls and former churches to buy. Once they have found a place, they refurbish it to a high level, kit it out with the latest technology, and turn it into a place of worship. Some of their buildings are undoubtedly impressive and its interior can psychologically have a positive effect on its members or on anyone visiting the church for the first time. Its 'wow' factor communicates that something good, important, or even 'big' is happening in the church, and they should be part of it. African churches are also likely to have good financial resources too, and able to offer opportunities that smaller churches cannot provide. Moreover, with their resources, they can put in place services, including, bible training institutes, concert and conference facilities, meeting places, nurseries, book, and coffee shops etc, that smaller churches may not be able to provide.

(4) 'Reverse Mission'

This is a concept prevalent among many African Christians, especially those from the *Redeemed Christian Church of God,* who see their mission in Britain as a reversal of the same way in which the missionaries once brought Christianity to Africa, and now so the argument goes, Britain is in need of re-evangelising. Many Africans see this as their Christian responsibility and are committed in doing so. One way in which they are doing this, is to 'aggressively' establish churches, so that today, especially in inner-city London, it's not unusual to see African churches flourishing in the capital as Indian corner shops once did.

Reverse mission also means proclaiming the gospel publicly as the early Caribbean used to, and every Saturday African Christians now hold regular 'open-air' services in many of the big shopping centres in London and the big cities. They are also spreading the word of God in the public space and overtly give their shops Christian names, *'God's Blessing Shop,' 'Abundant Life Shop, 'I Am' Services, 'Grace of God store,'* etc, as a way of proclaiming the gospel.

(5) African churches-use modern technology to grow their churches

African churches have a good grasp of modern communication and information technology and are generally on all the main social media platforms. They use technology and modern communication tools to grow their churches and attract young people to their services. They equip their churches with the latest PA systems, lighting and multimedia technology, and along with the latest musical instruments and facilities, provide a modern worship experience. They also use artistic expressions of worship including dance and drama, and many young people are beating a retreat to their services and want to be part of a modern church. African Christians, see solutions to problems rather than obstacles, and it's impossible to ignore the impact they are having on their members, and on their vision going forward. Cynics might say that this impact is largely 'in house,' and on African and Black people only, and not on British society.

While this may be so, what cannot be denied is the psychological impact they are having on the country and in their communities. Just look at any Sunday, and who do you see in large numbers any parish priest would envy, coming off trains, buses, and parking up their cars to go to church? While it may be true that not many white people will go into African churches, what cannot be denied, is that they know that they are there, they know locally, what they are doing is more for the good than the bad, and that's why I believe they are generally accepted. The reverse is also true if residents don't want an African church in their locality, they can be vocal in making their views known, as a few African church have found out to their cost.

(6) Africans market and promote their church-relentlessly

So much as changed today and social Media presents many possibilities for churches. African churches more than most, seem to grasp this and grasp the opportunities social media offers. You will find most African church have their own Websites, YouTube Channels, *stream* their services and are on all the main social media platforms. They know that almost anyone, especially the young, before visiting them are likely to have had an online experience of the church before going through the doors. As churches they also make good use of all the social media tools and use it extensively. For example, their members' posts throughout the services, *message and occasionally face-time.* They Tweet and use the search engines to make plain at any time during a service, anything they don't understand. Now that we have entered the area of *Podcasting*, African churches are right up there, adding to their ability to reach the unchurched and spread the gospel.

(7) Most African churches preach a prosperity doctrine

Most African church preach a prosperity doctrine which their members find aspirational and empowering. It's quite understandable that their members will aspire to 'the good life,' and have what others have in abundance. They use several scriptures to justify this.

And my God will supply all your needs according to his glorious riches in Christ Jesus. **Philippians 4:19**

But remember the LORD your God, for it is he who gives you the ability to produce wealth, and so confirms his covenant, which he swore to your ancestors, as it is today. **Deuteronomy 8:18**

But seek Ye first the kingdom of God and his righteousness, and all these things will be added to you. **Matthew 6:33**

A good man leaves an inheritance to his children's children, And the wealth of the sinner is stored up for the righteous. **Proverbs 13:22**

The last quote is a favourite, with often the second part of the verse quoted far more than the first. There is nothing wrong per se with acquiring wealth and riches providing the intention as Christians is to make good use of it. Secondly, both Africans and Caribbean have historically been denied the opportunity to make, create and access wealth, and it's therefore not surprising that they should seek to do so, now that they can.

(8) African churches are occupying the public space and partnering with Christian organisations

Kingsway International Christian Centre made a great impact when it was first launched in the 1990s and had extensive press coverage. In recent years, *The Redeemed Christian Church of God* has had both David Cameron, -the former British Prime Minister- and Prince Charles and the Duchess of Cornwall, at one of their services. Other African churches have had local representation. *Redeemed* strategy is to partner with some of the elite evangelical churches and para organisations, and this has helped to increase its profile. Today, *The Redeemed Christian Church of God* like most African churches are members of the Evangelical Alliance which is a white Christian organisation formed in 1846 which seeks to influence, the government, media, and society. Africans now hold senior positions within this organisation and are also represented in other para Christian and ecumenical groups, such as 'Christian Aid', 'Compassion', 'Tearfund' and 'Churches Together in Britain and Ireland'.

At the local level, African churches are also building strong links within their communities. *House on the Rock* in Archway Islington is an African church that is doing this. They are a good example of a church that hosts a variety of activities specifically aimed at people in their community, and people in Islington. They hold fetes in the summer, run a youth club, a food bank, hold gospel concerts, stage film and theatre evenings, and host a talent competition called, 'Islington's Got Talent'. New Wine Church in Woolwich South East London is another church that is doing similar things and is well known in their community.

THE CHALLENGES AFRICAN CHURCHES WILL FACE

U ndoubtedly African churches have made a huge impact on British society, and have completely changed the Black Pentecostal landscape in Britain, but what are some of the problems they are likely to face in the future. Like the Caribbean before they are now consolidating their position, and as they look to the future, there are areas of endeavours they'll have no control over, while others, their control will be minimal. It's going to take the wisdom of Solomon for African churches in practicing an orthodox Pentecostal Christianity, to navigate their way through what is an increasingly, secular and post-modernist society. Below are some of the problems I think they are likely to face.

"Reverse Mission' Will It Work

Many African Christians are passionate about 'reverse mission,' - the jury is out as to whether this can work, and there are several realities that might not make this as easy as it may sound. To start with, I'm not sure the average white person, Christian or non-Christian will necessarily take kindly to the idea that they need to be evangelised. As Brits, they are likely to say that they have their own Christianity, 'thank you very much, and are happy with it'. Moreover, as so much of religion in Britain is both class and culturally based, I'm not sure whether British people are ever going to take to, 'vibrant worship,' and what Black Pentecostals call, 'an encounter with God,'- perhaps not in the way that Black Pentecostals understand this. Overall, most white Christians are generally dismissive of Pentecostal and Evangelical Christianity, labelling it, 'happy-clappy' and emotionalism. Their Christianity perhaps emphasise a more 'rational' response, rather than 'an encounter with God', which to Pentecostals is an emotional outcome, no less effective, but an emotional response, nonetheless.

Perhaps all that African churches can realistically hope for in this area of ministry, is to be a lighthouse, a standard-bearer, a 'light set on a hill and with this, become an example for others and the nation to follow, rather than seek to 'convert' as the missionary once did, not always in a manner that's been historically useful to Black people, at all times, in all places and in all situations.

African churches also face an existential threat, for as Immigration in the UK falls, and as African and Caribbean make up less than 3% of the population; if African churches are to be successful in their desire to evangelise Britain, ('reverse mission,') they will need to attract white people into their churches. Pastor Agu Iruku who heads the Redeem Church of God in the UK, seems to accept this.

"I feel a church has to be open, has to reach out to all the groups wherever that church is – exactly what the missionaries did. London, especially, is a multicultural melting pot, and if a church is in London it should aim to look like London.
The Redeemed Christian Church of God has embarked on a radical programme of change. Society is changing rapidly. If

136

the church doesn't change too, it will be irrelevant in five to 10 years. We're going to chuck a lot of what we do because it just doesn't work." [34]

What will Africans take into the next generation

Another of the challenges African churches are likely to face in the future and one that has confronted Caribbean churches which unfortunately, they've not been able to solve, is how much of the African church tradition and worship experience will the next generation, of African young people retain and carry forward? I suspect, like many second, third and even fourth British Caribbean, the next generation of Africans are likely to reject many of their parent's religious practices and seek out new contemporary expressions of worship. Just as the Caribbean before, unless African churches devise plans to keep their young people in their churches, and can keep them from being 'overwhelmed' by the increasing secularization of British society, then they are likely to go the same way as Caribbean young people, who now have left the church or is seeking new expressions of Christianity, and not necessarily, ones, based on their parents or grandparents religion.

Second and subsequent generation of Africans live and will continue to live a very different life to their parents, and their values, outlook and expectation will naturally and mainly be shaped by the society in which they live and are growing up in. How subsequent generations of Africans will navigate this, is the challenge many will face. The signs are already there, as African millennials are increasingly looking away from their parent's church and seeking out multicultural and multi-ethnic churches and are beginning to flock there.

Cultural Identity

In my other book, *'How to make gospel music work for you,'* I advise gospel artists when starting out, that one of the first things, they should be clear on is the identity of their music for this is what people will buy into. I think something similar can be said about African churches for so many lacks a distinct cultural identity. I know many deliberately don't foster this, but how often have I sat in an African church, and hadn't I known that this was a Nigerian or Ghanaian church, I'd have no idea, where I am. I'd know that it is a Black Pentecostal church for its spiritual and theological identity would be clear, but culturally less so. I may glean from the clothes some of the people wear, but it's likely to be a few. You'd think that the music, the language or the liturgy would culturally locate it, but again you're likely to be disappointed. Perhaps, the time you're likely to get a cultural expression, which is when I got mine, is when a baby was being Christened. I suppose the reason is because this is such an important ritual, part of the general naming ceremony which probably predates Christianity, and so is expressed culturally. I hear the same is also true for weddings and funerals, but It's disappointing that these are likely to be the only times.

Unfortunately, today, so many cultural expressions are sacrificed on the altar of modernity, multi-ethnic and multi-racial imperative in African services, that it leaves a cultural vacuum. Identity is everything, whether spiritual or cultural, for it is consciousness- the belief in who we are, and not who we think we should be or would like to be. Thankfully, young Africans in the secular world seemed to be grasping this, and through their writings and music are beginning to reclaim their heritage in new and exciting ways.

Single Women and Gender Imbalance

This issue has dodge Caribbean churches for ages-what to do about singleness, largely women within the churches. Black women historically have been the backbones of the Black Pentecostal church and there has always been a gender imbalance. Disproportionately, there are more women in the churches than men, and over the years this has become more pronounced to the point that unless this is addressed, it will soon become a crisis. While specifically there may not be any data on this as it relates to women in African churches, anecdotally the trend is likely to mirror that of Caribbean women.

From an analysis of the Labour Force Survey (2004-8), Platt found that 65 per cent of Black British women from African Caribbean backgrounds are without a partner as compared to 23 per cent of Indian and Pakistani British women. Additional analysis indicates that the largest ethnic group of never-married women are Black Caribbean women; 57 per cent as compared with other groups such as Asian women who have a never-married rate of approximately 10 per cent (Jayaweera et al., 2007). In America, the issue is no less different with 42 per cent of African American women remaining unmarried, compared to only 23 per cent of Caucasian women. (Yale Study) [35]

The evidence seems to suggest that singleness in the church is already a problem and is likely to continue to be so in the future. Anecdotally we know this already which means that something needs to be done for obvious reasons and that the church needs to devise strategies to deal with this.

Part of the problem is how to attract more men into churches and how to encourage them to become members. Also, as Christian women choice of partners becomes limited, they may want to extend their choice of a mate outside the church, but here in lies the problem-certainly for Caribbean Christians-, for they are in danger of violating one of the most often quoted scripture on this subject. I'm not sure, however, whether it has anything specifically to do with choosing a partner or marriage.

Do not be unequally yoked together with unbelievers. For what [a] fellowship has righteousness with lawlessness? And what [b]communion has light with darkness? (Corinthians 6 v 14)

The traditional Caribbean Pentecostal interpretation of this scripture seems to restrict and limit the choice women can make in this area. It is the one most often quoted to deter a woman from making a choice of a mate outside the church and is the one that presents her with the greatest dilemma. The church now needs to clarify Paul instruction on this and explain whether he was speaking about possible marriage partners, for this begs the question, can two Christians be unequally yoked, or put another way, are all Christians who are married, equally yoked?

Charismatic Leader

Many Black Pentecostal Church have a strong charismatic leader, and with this, there is always the danger that if the leader leaves whether due to a disagreement, retirement, death or even a scandal, the church may be in danger of not surviving as so much of the identity of the church is tied up, embodied or invested in the charisma and personality of the leader. Even when in churches structures are put in place to ensure accountability and as checks and balances, the sheer force and personality of the leader can be such, that they may be rendered ineffective. Churches who are part of a larger organisation, rather than an independent one, have a much better chance of surviving its leader if there is a problem, as the whole is likely to be greater than its constituent parts. Smaller churches also stand a much better chance of surviving the demise of a leader as they are less likely to rely on the leader and more on its members. It's likely that these smaller churches have long-standing families who are the backbone of the church and embodies the will and identity of it, and so able to weather the storm, whereas a leader leaving a large church, is likely to leave a large hole in it, simply because of the size of the leader's personality.

Unfortunate Headlines

'Church directors earn between £60,000 and £80,000 each.

'A typical Church of England vicar earns around £21,500'

The Archbishop of Canterbury, who has responsibility for an active congregation of close to a million people, only earns £68,740 a year'. (The Guardian 2009)

'Forbes magazine estimates the fortunes of Nigeria's five richest pastors. Oyedepo topped the list, with an estimated net worth of $150 million'.
(Reuter 2011)

These are some of the press headlines' in recent years and African churches can do best to avoid them for they will undermine the effect and influence they are having on British society. The British tend to downplay wealth, unlike America, who celebrates it. This is just a cultural difference but an important one. Also, increase public wealth and profile, invariably leads and attract, increase forensic media scrutiny!

Small is beautiful

Not everyone likes a big church, and many prefer the intimacy of a small congregation. One of the disadvantages of a large church is that it can lack adequate personal pastoral care, even though there may be structures in place for it. A large church can sometimes feel impersonal and can make people feel isolated, or even a stranger. In a small church, people tend to feel more 'connected' to each other and get to know and appreciate each other, whereas in a big church this is likely to be more difficult. In a small church also, people who want to serve are more likely to be given a chance to do so, whereas, in a large church they may have to wait for an opportunity to arise, or may need to have the required qualifications to even be considered. Large churches can also be cliquey, making newcomers feel like outsiders and that they don't belong.

This is not to suggest that one type of church is better than the other or a small church is better than a large one, or visa versa as both have their advantages and disadvantages. It's down to personal choice, and the point here is to draw attention to some of the misgivings and belief that a church that is growing exponentially is an indication of God's blessing, and by implication, a small church is outside of His grace. For many, small will always be beautiful!

TWO DIFFERENT PATHS

AFRICAN AND CARIBBEAN PATHS

The high point of British gospel music was the 1980s, when several artists were signed to major record labels. Gospel was on national radio, there was a thriving gospel music circuit, American gospel artists were regular visitors, and gospel was in the West -End and in the churches. While all this was happening, several changes were also taking place.

The internet and social media were being introduced, digital technology was transforming the way music was made, African churches were coming into their own, and although the country had slipped into recession, not since 'the golden age of gospel music' was so much gospel being produced in Britain.

Today, African gospel artists now lead the way in British gospel music, dominating it in much the same way Caribbean artists once did. But there are signs of a parting of the ways. Why is this, what has caused this change? or put another way, why has African and Caribbean gospel not developed along the same lines? One of the reasons I believe is the way in which the two groups (African and Caribbean) came to gospel music in the first place.

Historically, Caribbean came to gospel music as a result of, *'Oh Happy Day'* and more importantly, the range of R&B gospel artists they were exposed to. Secondly, there is a cultural similarity between American gospel R&B and West Indian church music, and that's why gospel music was readily accepted in Caribbean churches. Africans, on the other hand, came to the music another way, mainly through the wave of white American Evangelical preachers, who went out to Africa in the 1980s and 90s and brought along with them their worship leaders and their 'praise and worship' songs! *'Praise and Worship'* artists, like Don Moen, Ron Kennoly, Paul Baloche, Paul Wilbur and many of the artists on the Hosanna music label, simply stepped into this growing market and created a demand for it. That's why, a prominent African worship leader once said to me, *'Praise and worship'* will always take preference in African churches over R&B gospel, because it's the music Africans came to Christ with, and as such it occupies a special place in their hearts!

With this understanding, three things are now clear. One is that the *'Praise and Worship'* artists that have largely influenced Africans introduction to gospel music, differs sharply from R&B gospel, and the course their music is taking, differs from Caribbean also. Secondly, I now understand why African churches are preoccupied with *'praise and worship'* in the way that Caribbean churches are not, although this is changing. Thirdly, I also now understand why the music of, Matt Redman, Tim Hughes and other British 'worship artists,' translate so easily into African churches, often at the expense of their indigenous music, and don't translate that easily in Caribbean churches, although again this is changing. I only realise the latter when I attended a conference at a traditional Caribbean church and was surprised that in the worship part of the conference, all the songs were composed by *'praise and worship'* artists, and not a single one, was either a hymn, a Caribbean chorus or an American gospel song. I wondered if I was witnessing the future!

UNDERSTANDING BRITISH GOSPEL MUSIC

Any understanding of the role African artists and their church now plays in British gospel music necessitates an understanding of the history of the music itself, as British gospel music is deeply rooted in a Black Pentecostal church tradition, and it's from there that it draws its inspiration and strength. Historically, the early form of the music is West Indian church music, and it's from there that it has grown and developed. In the 1960s it was the music of second-generation West Indians, and in the 70s and 80s, the music came under the influence of American gospel music. Of all the American gospel artists who have influenced West Indian church music, *Edwin Hawkins, James Cleveland, Andrae Crouch and The Winans,* have had the greatest impact. *Edwin Hawkins,* because of *Oh Happy Day, James Cleveland,* because of his enormous influence on the gospel choral sound, *Andrae Crouch* because he was the first genuine international artist of the modern age, and *The Winans* because of their influenced on urban gospel and for bringing a new and younger crowd to the music.

EDWIN HAWKINS, (1943-2018) impact on British gospel music came as a result of his re-working of an old church hymn, *Oh Happy Day that Fixed my Choice,* which every West Indian Christian knew because it's an old hymn sang at 'altar call' and baptismal services. In 1969 as *Oh Happy Day,* this song became a huge international hit and topped the

145

music charts around the world reaching number 4 in America, number 2 in Britain, and number 1 in France and Germany. It sold over seven million copies when it was released, and as the song was out of copyright, Edwin Hawkins was able to claim all the rights to it, as well as all the revenue.

What *Oh Happy Day* showed was that the music that began on the plantations of the American south had become a global phenomenon. It was now on television on Top of the Pops in Britain, on the radio, in the news, in magazines and newspapers all over the world. On the back of this, several British record companies in the 1980s thought the next music would be gospel and went out to Black Pentecostal churches to look for gospel choirs who could replicate what Edwin had done fifteen years earlier! It's no coincidence that both *The London Community Gospel Choir* and *The Inspirational Choir* were signed to major record labels at that time.

JAMES CLEVELAND (1931-1991) is a monumental figure in gospel music, and his name will forever be synonymous with gospel choirs and the gospel choral sound that he more than any other, helped to create. British gospel choirs were big fans of James Cleveland, and most choirs patterned their style of gospel singing on his choir and routinely sang his songs. In the 1980s, Cleveland came to Britain for a series of television shows including a Granada ITV Special. This was the moment Cleveland's army of British gospel fans was waiting for, to get a chance to see the great man and his world-famous choir. Unfortunately, Cleveland didn't have the opportunity to work directly with any British gospel choir, but that didn't diminish his influence or the effect he had on British gospel music.

ANDRAE CROUCH (1942-2015), has had the greatest influence on present-day gospel music perhaps more than any other modern gospel artist, and gospel music owes a lot to him. Andréa's gospel was music for a modern age and yet was deeply rooted in a Black gospel tradition. Andréa's gospel music is all about an enjoyable Christianity, and all his songs reflect this theme. Examples of these are: *Take Me Back, Soon and Very Soon, The Blood Will Never Lose its Power, through it All, Oh It Is Jesus and I Don't Know Why Jesus Loves Me.* Andrae was a frequent visitor to Britain coming to do concerts and television performances. His influence on British gospel music is colossal, and in 1999 he made his last television appearance in Britain on a BBC Songs of Praise programme which I produced.

THE WINANS was Andréa Crouch protégés and when they burst onto the gospel music scene in 1983, they were sensational. The Winans helped to popularise a new form of gospel music - Urban Gospel - which sent the music off in a new and exciting direction. They were a male gospel group, not a choir. They were slick, stylish, good-looking, modern, could sing, wrote great songs, had gospel and R & B appeal, and yet were every bit Black Pentecostal church! British gospel fans loved them, and every gospel group in the 1980s wanted to be like the Winans, and every female fan had their 'favourite' Winans!

In the 1980s, when African Christians started arriving in Britain, the music in Black Pentecostal churches was led by Caribbean artists and musicians. Both the *London Community Gospel Choir and The Inspirational Choir* led by Bazil Meade and John Francis respectively, were at the forefront of this and were the two best examples of this new type of music

THE LONDON COMMUNITY GOSPEL CHOIR (LCGC)

The London Community Gospel Choir was started by Bazil Meade, Lawrence Johnson, Delroy Powell, and my brother, John Francis. The original idea was for a gospel community choir, for a one-off concert in May 1983 at Kensington Temple, in Notting Hill Gate, West London. The concert was an amazing success and invitations to perform followed.

At first, Bazil was reluctant to continue any further than the one concert, but the reaction of the public, the media and the young people in his charge persuaded him to carry on. As the choir's popularity grew, many of the church leaders objected to what Bazil was doing, performing in secular venues, and they didn't take kindly to him taking their young people unsupervised there also. For some pastors, this was a step too far, and as many of the choir members came from different churches, this presented a huge problem. Bazil, however, decided to run with his vision and see where God would lead him. This idea of an inter-denominational choir was something new to the Black Pentecostal church community, and many church leaders felt threatened by it".

We knew this was a vision that God had given us, and that inspired us to keep going despite the controversy which surrounded us. Bazil Meade – 'A Boy, A Journey, A Dream'. (Monarch Books)

For 35 years, Bazil has led The London Community Gospel Choir and today they are a household name and the nation's favourite gospel choir. They've also become the training ground for many up-and-coming gospel artists, singers and musicians, with many first cutting their teeth in the choir and have since gone on to great things. In 2018, Bazil was awarded an MBE in recognition for the contribution he's made to British Gospel Music. Trevor Phillips, the former head of the Equality and Human Rights Commission, writing in Bazil's book, eloquently sums up his contribution.

"Bazil didn't invent gospel music, but he made it British and transformed our parents' private music into a passionate public expression of the spirited heart of the Black community."

JOHN FRANCIS AND THE INSPIRATIONAL CHOIR

Unlike the London Community Gospel choir which consisted of members from different churches, the Inspirational choir belonged to one church, – *'The Pentecostal First Born Church of the Living God,'* in Islington North London, one of the early West Indian churches that started life in Britain in the 1950s. The choir was formed by John Francis after he attended a Church Convention in Waycross Georgia, and while there met Douglas Miller, a gospel artist, who encouraged him to start a choir when he got back to London, which he duly did.

The next stage in the *The Inspirational Choir's* development came in 1982 when the choir recorded *'Wings of a Dove'* with *'Madness'*, the 1980s, controversial pop group. From there the choir went on to sign to 'Stiff Records' and released their first EP single. A national tour with radio and television exposure followed, and the choir was soon in demand and quickly built up a reputation as a 'must-see' live act. In 1984, the choir signed to CBS (today's Sony Music), releasing three singles and album, 'Sweet Inspiration' with the hit single, *Abide with Me.* CBS was excited about this track and got members of the London Philharmonic Orchestra and the Royal Choral Society to perform on it. The track was scheduled for the Christmas market, and when it was released, *Abide with Me* quickly took off, thanks mainly to the late Terry Wogan, who played it regularly on his Radio 2 Morning Show. Unfortunately, CBS was caught unaware and didn't have enough copies of *Abide with Me* in the shops. To make matters worse it was Christmas and all the pressing plants were closed for the holidays. The result was, the track was lost, and *Abide with Me* only reached number 36 in the national charts, when it was a potential top 10!

Not everyone agreed with the direction CBS took with the choir and when the album *Sweet Inspiration* was released, it received mixed reviews. The main criticism was the album was thought to be 'middle of the road' and although its general thrust was traditional gospel, the lush strings, and choral arrangements on some of the tracks, were not to everyone's liking. Whatever the rights or wrongs of the direction CBS took, the choir signing to them was a major achievement as it opened doors both for them and for British gospel music. It also gave John a platform from which to start his ministry, and although the choir is now long disbanded and no more, echoes of them can still be heard at Ruach City Church in South London, where John is the pastor. It's all a far cry from a humble beginning, that started in a small church at 71 White Lion Street in Islington North London.

BRITISH GOSPEL MUSIC-PAST PRESENT AND THE FUTURE

With both The London Community Gospel Choir and the Inspirational choir leading the way in the 1980s, gospel music seemed to be everywhere during this decade and epitomised how far the music had come. Gospel was regularly on the radio, it was on television, in churches and concert halls. It was in the West End in the musicals of *'Amen Corner'* the James Baldwin play. It was in *'King,'* based on the life of the great man, and in *'Mama I want to Sing,'* which charted the life of Doris Troy, from her humble church background to Broadway. Dawn Thomas, a British gospel artist appeared in the British production, and I played a part in helping to bring it to London and the West End.

In the 1980s, Gospel was also on Radio 1 with Gary Byrd and his weekly gospel show *'Sweet Inspiration.'* Al Matthew was playing it on Capital FM, and Dave 'P' presented the main gospel programme on Choice FM. In North London, Brother Michael Francis (no relation) was playing gospel, and outside the capital, Dulcie Dixon was playing it at Radio Leicester, so was John McPherson at radio Sheffield, and the late Frank Stewart was on BBC WM in Birmingham. You could also hear gospel if you listened carefully, for it was in the music and songs of, *James Brown, Aretha Franklin, Stevie Wonder, The Supremes, The Temptations, Marvin Gaye, Smokey Robinson, Al Green, Curtis Mayfield, The Staple Singers* and virtually every Motown artist who dominated the airways at that time. What's more, these artists in the interview they gave would frequently make mention of their church and gospel upbringing, and in so doing, add to the sense that gospel was everywhere in Britain at that time.

GOSPEL ON TELEVISION

Television also played its part in generating an interest in gospel music during the *Golden Age*. At one time or the other, there were three gospel music shows on British television. *Pop Gospel* made by Granada Television was the first, and what *Pop Gospel* tried to do was to showcase the music of white Christian artists like Bryn Haworth and Garth Hewitt. It wasn't a huge success, and in 1984, the BBC launched its own series, *'The Rock Gospel Show'* which was presented by Sheila Walsh - a former missionary and Alvin Stardust, a 70s pop star in his own right.

The Rock Gospel Show was loosely based on the hugely successful *Top of the Pops* chart show, and its main aim was to showcase contemporary Christian music to a mainstream television audience. The problem with *The Rock Gospel Show* was that it had more 'rock' than gospel, as well as being a pale imitation of *Top of the Pops* the show it was trying to imitate. As a result, it was heavily criticised both within and outside the Christian community, for among other things, not being clear on what it was doing musically. For example, it failed to capture the spirit, enthusiasm, and excitement of the type of gospel people were listening to, hearing on the radio, seeing on their television, and increasingly becoming accustomed to.

Eventually the show was dropped, and a few years later a new gospel series appeared on British television, but what is not generally known, is the genesis of this new show.

BBC SONGS OF PRAISE

The new show which dominated the religious airways in the 1980s was 'People Get Ready,' and it has its origins in BBC 'Songs of Praise.' As a religious television programme, *'Songs of Praise'* has been going for over 60 years. During the 1980s it played a vital part in bringing Black gospel music to a mainstream television audience. It was once a big programme with a huge audience and would regularly pull in 7+ million viewers. It was on every Sunday evening immediately after the early evening news, and was for many people, the nation's alternative to going to church or, as one critic put it, 'the country's religious moment.'

On Sunday 26th February 1984, *Songs of Praise* broadcast an unusual programme from Southwark Cathedral. The programme, *A Celebration of Gospel,* was presented by Geoffrey Wheeler and produced by Christopher Mann. Along with its regular diet of hymns and interviews, *A Celebration of Gospel* also explored the background of gospel music and featured some well-known gospel songs. The congregation was predominantly Black - a first for the programme - and featured the late Sam King who was one of the original passengers on the *Empire Windrush* who arrived in Britain in 1948. By 1984 Sam King had become Britain's first Black Mayor and the Mayor of Southwark!

A *Celebration of Gospel* was a big hit with the audience and *Songs of Praise* department received one of its biggest post-bags to date. It was a watershed moment in the history of British Gospel Music and as a result, Channel 4 commissioned TVS (Television South) to produce a gospel music series.

PEOPLE GET READY

The result of Channel 4 Commission was *'People Get Ready'* which was made by Television South - formerly part of the ITV Network. Andrew Barr, a former *Songs of Praise* senior producer, along with Peter Williams-Head of Religious Programmes at TVS, was in charge of the series. Andrew chose a young South African, the late Frances Tulloch to produce the initial programmes and *People Get Ready* was successful for many reasons. One was the partnership between TVS, and the gospel community which Andrew brought to the series. The production team was made up of members of both and what the series aimed to do was to capture the 'spirit' of a gospel church/concert event. Rather than have any preconceived ideas on how to achieve this, Andrew relied on the advice from those of us on the production team, while he and his programme-makers concentrated on the technical aspect of making the programmes, exciting, authentic and as true as possible to the music.

People Get Ready production team consisted of, the late Frances Tulloch, Viv Broughton, Nicky Brown, Peter Toms, John Francis (presenter), Juliet Coley (presenter) and me. As part of the production team, we had a lot of freedom in helping to shape the direction and content of each programme, and what we were all trying to do was to bring the excitement and experience of a gospel church service, to a television audience.

154

Each programme centred on John, the singer/preacher who presented the programmes from his Hammond organ, while Juliet Coley - Sister J - did the more formal television links and interviews along with a short comedy spot in the earlier programmes. All the programmes included a gospel choir, a group, a soloist, a short interview, and the late Lavine Hudson, the resident vocalist, brought each programme to a close with a big gospel number. Frances thought a lot of Lavine and was excited when she signed to Virgin Records as Lavine was being touted by the record business, as Britain's answer to Witney Houston. Frances believed that with Lavine's projected success, it would rub off on the series and help to make it a success also.

People Get Ready produced great live gospel music and used the best musicians from the gospel community. It added a top horn section to add colour and texture, and each programme featured the best home-grown talent chosen from a series of nationwide auditions which I conducted throughout the country. When I started to produce the programmes, the format was extended to include American gospel artists, to give the series an international feel. *Shirley Caesar, The Williams Brothers, Tramaine Hawkins, the late Thomas Whitfield, The Oslo Gospel Choir and Larnelle Harris,* all appeared on the show.

No amount of money was spared in making *People Get Ready* a success and TVS brought in a top Light Entertainment Director, and invested heavily on the set, lighting and sound. The series was hugely successful within the Black church community and today it's fondly remembered and highly spoken of.

Channel 4 went on to commission as part of the package of programmes, *A Christmas Gospel Special* and an original, Gospel Oratorio- *Creation* which was staged and filmed at the Marlowe Theatre in Canterbury.

People Get Ready was ahead of its time and if a criticism can be levied at the series today which is easy with experience and hindsight, is that we should have 'educated' the audience a bit more on the music we were presenting, as most of it was unfamiliar to them. The gospel audience knew all the songs, understood the religious content of each programme and was happy with it, but to a mainstream television audience, most of what we were presenting, was largely unknown.

THE GOSPEL MARKET TODAY

Like all commercial music, gospel operates in a marketplace. A market in the literal sense of the term is any place where buyers and sellers meet to trade. It could be on the high street, part of an exhibition, at a church, a conference, at a gospel concert or even on the web. In this sense, there has always been a market for gospel music in Britain. The sellers were once mainly Caribbean, consisting of several small independent 'gospel music traders' who would do the rounds of church services, conferences, conventions and gospel concerts, where they'd sell their CDs, books and Christian artefacts. The market was essentially the Caribbean Pentecostal church community, historically small, and operated mainly on an ad hoc basis. It was largely uncontrolled, lacked any organisational structure, had no meaningful support or any real investment, and was mostly hidden. It operated within 'church walls,' and *Spirit Music and Crossway Music* were two examples of businesses that operated and were well known in this market. In general, the market continued and remained largely the same until around the mid-90s, when Send the Light (STL) and its network of Wesley Owen retail book shops, came on the market and changed everything.

For twelve years, gospel music had a good friend on the high street with STL being the supplier of Christian music including gospel, as well as a retail outlet. In 2009, STL collapsed and with it, its 41 Wesley Owen bookshops. One effect of this failure was that paradoxically it led to Black Pentecostal Churches setting up their own in-house bookshops, reflecting a need in their churches and in the growth in their numbers.

Today, the Black Pentecostal church community is the market for gospel music, the natural home for it, and the place where gospel artists are likely to find success. More gospel music is being produced in Britain today than at any time, and the market is lively and buoyant. African artists now represent the most significant area of growth, and African churches now provide the main market for the music. It's not surprising for African churches have the largest congregations, offer the main audience for the music, and with their numbers growing exponentially, they will continue to dominate the music and the market for years to come.

What every gospel artist should now be doing with their music is targeting it to the African church community for it's there that they'll find the best support for it. Many artists might not believe this and believe that they should aim their music at the general music market, or even to the White Christian community, believing that this is where they will find success. If they do, they are likely to be disappointed, for both markets are too broad and lack enough buyers who are actively looking for music that UK gospel artists are producing for them to be successful. Moreover, as most music today is niche, success is likely to be found in these markets, rather than in large ones.

Today, gospel music like all music is gravitating online, but this is only part of the story, for as access to the music has changed, so too has the market for it. African artists now represent the most significant area of growth, and African churches are now the dominant force. It's not surprising, for they have the largest congregations, offer the main audience for the music, and with their numbers growing exponentially, the interest in the music is likely to continue.

'Praise and Worship' is the main music in African churches today and this will continue to dominate, especially as new upgraded versions of it are being produced every day by gospel artists coming out of the multi-racial and multi-cultural churches in America. African artists too are adding to this, as *Sinach, Nathaniel Bassey* and others are doing with their brand of 'African worship songs.' It's likely that Caribbean churches will follow as many are already doing, mainly because, and if for no other reason, success breeds success, and as African churches are seen to be 'successful,' they'll become a magnet, and draw in who they will.

DECLINING STANDARDS?

With the advance in music production, technology and social media, anyone today can make gospel music and have it available to the public. The downside however is that with anyone able to do so, it's inevitable that standards will fall. In the past, record companies were the filter of the music, deciding on whose music the public would hear. Today this is no longer the case, for anyone now can make an album and call themselves a gospel artist. In other words, there's no objective standard or a required level of competence, and as a result, this leads to declining standards. The ultimate judge I suppose is the consumer or the market, and as most gospel artists music doesn't sell anyway, I suppose this is the 'market' sifting out the good from the bad. Also, as cream always rise to the top, good music will ultimately prevail, and the rest will sink to the bottom or drift away.

PARTING OF THE WAYS?

I believe there will be a parting of the ways and that British gospel music will divide into African and Caribbean, and I think its already doing so. It's also likely that with *'Praise and Worship'* the default music in African churches, Caribbean gospel artists are likely to take a different route with their music, seeing it not so much in the Black Pentecostal churches in the UK, but outside into the wider music world. *The London Community Gospel Choir, Kingdom Choir, and Ken Burton* and his two choirs are leading the way in this, propelling their music to the wider marketplace and will continue to do so.

Other Caribbean artists are seeing the European Christian market as the place where they are likely to find success with their music and are pitching it there. *Carla Jane, New Ye, John Fisher and IDMC, Colin Vassell, Lurine Cato, Peter Francis and Wayne Ellington* are already doing this, and are good examples of British Caribbean artists who now have a following in Christian Communities in Europe, and are building on this and pursuing their ministry there.

I believe that although the two music, African and Caribbean may initially diverge, they can also exist side by side and in time may converge and draw from each other. They don't need to be exclusive of each other, as both are coming to the music from the same standpoint but responding to the demands of it in different ways. This is not necessarily a bad thing, especially as so much music today is niche, and the world is becoming more and more a global village. Perhaps now more than ever, people are looking for new creative ways to serve God and express their faith, and gospel music can help in this, but the custodians of the music will need to play their part, making sure that the music continues to operate at the highest level, and that artist remain true to one of the greatest music ever.

APPENDICES

References

1- London the place for me-Lord Kitchener

2- The New Republic Magazine-Interview with Trevor Philips by Kaila Philo-June 22 2018

3- Windrush: Who exactly was on board? Lucy Rodgers & Maryam Ahmed: BBC News 21 June 2001)

4- Windrush Stories-British Library
   How Caribbean migrants helped to rebuild Britain-Linda McDowell-4 Oct 2018

5- The history of Black people in Britain- Paul Edwards | Published in History Today Volume 31 Issue 9 September 1981 The New Republic: The Caribbean Immigrants Who Transformed Britain By Kaila Philo.

6- Forces War Records: Unit History- British West Indian Regiment www.Forces-war-records.co.uk, 139 (Jamaican) Squadron Pathfinders: www.rafupwood.co.uk/139lossesin1944.htm

7- Windrush West Indians fought for Britain in war-David Smith - The Guardian 8th June 2008)

8- BBC-Bitesize-Britain and the Caribbean -National 5
   https:/ www.bbc.co.uk/bitesize/guides/zjyqtfr/revision/2

9- The Great Smog of London -Wikipedia

10- ibid

11- Donni McClurken-Live in London-Release 17th August 2000 Record Label, Verity Records 2000 (01241-43150-2) Zomba Recording LLC 2-D

12- A brief history of Christian music-Andrew Wilson Dickson

13- ibid

14- ibid

15- Sampson, Cheryl A. (January 2015) 'Hymn Lining: -A Black Church Tradition with Roots in Europe' The Spectrum: A Scholar's Day Journal, Vol 3, Article 9

16- Bletson, D (2009, March 28) Church of God in Christ (1907) www.blackpast.org/african-american-history/church-god christ-1907/

17- He has brought us a mighty long way' Caribbean Pentecostal Churches in Britain by Dr R David Muir

18- Respect-Understanding British Caribbean Christianity-p93 Joe Aldred-

19- COGOP Biannual Report

20- Y William G Johnsson
This article was first printed in the February 8, 2001, issue of the Adventist Review. For more information on the Adventist Church in Great Britain

21- This Date in History, March 1, 1954, London Crusade begins The Billy Graham Library -March 1st 2013

22- The Billy Graham Library, Crusade City Spotlight: London, August 3

23- 2012: https//billygrahamlibrary.org/crusade-city-spotlight-

24- ibid

25- Where Do I Go from Here? Jim Reeves (1923-1964)
From the album-We Thank Thee

26- When God Dips, His Love in My Heart- Tennessee Ernie Ford
(Cleavant Derricks 1910-1977) 40 Treasured Hymns.

27- Swing Low, Sweet Chariot- Steve Rouse-programme notes:
Manhattan Beach Music) (2)

28- www.twainquotes.com

29- 'Speak of me as I Am'-The Black presence in Southwark since
1600-Southwark Council 2005

30- A History of Hymns-Precious Lord Take My Hand-Printed in
'Discipleship Ministries-C Michael Hawn

31- An Illustrated History of Gospel-Steve Turner

32- Being built together-the story of Black Majority Churches in
Southwark-University of Roehampton

33- What the London Church Census reveals- Peter Brierley

34- Pentecostal Church Looks to White Britons to Boost
Congregation (The Guardian)

35- It is not good to be alone; singleness and the Black Seventh-day
Adventist Woman: Valerie Y. Bernard-Allan PhD thesis-Institute
of Education- University College London. UCL

Glossary

Accept Christ as Personal Saviour
A person in a Pentecostal church choosing to commit to becoming a Christian.

Alter Call
This is the part in a Pentecostal Church Service when a person is invited to commit to Christ. They usually show this by going to the Alter at the front of a church where they'd be prayed for, and this act signifies that they've become a Christian and is then accepted as part of the broader Christian community.

13 Amendment 1865
This Amendment to the American Constitution legally abolished 'slavery and involuntary servitude'

Born Again
This is Pentecostal speak for becoming a Christian which is a deliberate act of will in which a person agrees to 'accept Christ as a personal Saviour' and agrees to live and follows his teaching.

Bringing the Word/Delivery the Message
A sermon-call to preach.

Colour Bar

An unofficial social system that existed in some parts of Britain in the 1960s when Black and Asian were 'barred' from certain places.

Call to be Saved

The same as accepting Christ as a personal saviour.

Civil Rights Movement

This was a movement in America during the 1950s and 60s when Black people fought for social justice and equality in American society. The springboard was Rosa Parks -a Black woman who refused to give up her seat at the front of the bus she was travelling in to a white man, as the segregation laws of Alabama dictated. Rosa Parks was arrested and a young Baptist Minister –Martin Luther King- was asked to lead a boycott of the bus company. This incident ignited the general struggle for equality and justice under the law for Black people in America

Campground Meetings

These were secret meeting usually some distance from the slave master's house where the slaves would meet to sing, dance and shout in their own African way. They sang and dance to share the pain of their enslavement and to hope for a time when they would be free. The slave would 'ring shout' where they would gather in a circle, and sing, shout, clap their hands, dance and chant ecstatically often ending up in a trance. The singing from these campground meetings was the precursor of the 'Spirituals.'

Call and Response

Call and Response is what it says- one musical phrase (call) is followed by another (the response). This is a tradition that began in slavery and was a feature of the songs that slave sang as they worked. Today "Call and Response" is expressed in many ways- in religious gatherings, Western church music (Antiphony), Pentecostal services-'can I get an Amen,' sports gatherings and in a multiple of music forms-in gospel, blues, jazz, R&B and hip-hop.

Billy Graham Crusade

These were the meetings or church services Billy Graham conducted throughout the world. They were called Crusade because Billy Graham saw his mission as fighting against sin/ evil/wickedness/darkness and bringing people to Christ free from sin and into the light.

Doxology

Doxology is an expression of praise to God in Christian worship. In West Indian Pentecostal churches this signals the end of the service and is often the final song before the benediction-the blessing. A typical doxology in West church services is: 'Praise God from whom all blessings flow, praise Him all creatures here below, praise, praise Him above the heaven and the earth, praise father son and holy ghost-Amen' In contemporary Christianity, 'Gloria Excelsis' is a well-known doxology.

Diocese

Diocese is a district or parish under the pastoral care of a bishop in the Christian Church.

Devil Music

The blues historically in America is known as 'devil's music' mainly because of its long association with the lifestyle and music of a section of Black America during the 1900s with the establishment of Juke joints (clubs), speakeasies (an illegal drinking club during prohibition), creep joints (brothels) Ragtime(the for runner of jazz) and barrelhouse jazz. As far back as 1800, the word 'blue' was slang for being drunk and therefore the religious part of Black America disapproved of the music coming out of these places as devil music.'

Devotional Service

In West Indian churches this refers to the first part of the service-the more formal part. It's usually characterised by a hymn, prayer and scripture reading.

'Empire Windrush'

'SS Empire Windrush' was a former German cruise boat that was used to transport the first batch of West Indians to Britain to help in the reconstruction of the country after world war 2 .

Emancipation Proclamation 1863

This was the declaration issued by President Lincoln that 'all persons held as slaves within any State or designated part of a State...shall be and forever free.' This did not in itself abolished slavery that came with the 13th Amendment.

Enoch Powell (1921-1998)

Enoch Powell was an influential British Conservative politician and a former Minister of Health and Shadow Defence Secretary. On April 20th, 1968 he made a speech to the Conservative Association in Birmingham which the press dubbed 'Rivers of blood.' In the speech, he criticised immigration to Britain from the Commonwealth and the government's proposed legislation of Race Relations. Powell said that as he looked ahead that he was filled with 'foreboding. Like the Roman, I seem to see "the River Tiber foaming with much blood". He was sacked from the Conservative Front Bench by Edward Heath, the Conservative leader for being inflammatory and liable to damage race relations.

Grip

A suitcase. Many West Indians had a suitcase packed from the moment they arrived in Britain for their eventual return home.

Gospel Train

The Gospel Train is a famous spiritual. It was first published in 1872 and became one of the songs of the Fisk Jubilee Singers. Like most spirituals the words/lyrics had a dual meaning. On the surface it alludes to Christian imagery and meaning but it was also coded language which slaves used to signal escapes to freedom.

" The gospel train is coming
I hear it just at hand
I hear the car wheels moving
And rumbling through the land
Get on board, children (3×)
For there's room for many a more

Holiness Churches

In the early 1900s a radical form of Protestant Christianity emerged in America as Pentecostals whose central principle is the day of Pentecost which in the bible is the Jewish festival of weeks. Both Charles Parham (1873-1929) and William James Seymour (1870-1922) an African American were the principle people behind this movement with the Azusa Street

Revival Meetings in Los Angeles California (1906-1915) started by Seymour, is credited with igniting the worldwide interest in Pentecostalism. Pentecostals emphasise a person's relationship with God through baptism in the holy spirit and the speaking in tongues.

Holy Ghost
holy spirit

Jubilee
Jubilee in the Old Testament in the bible refers to the ownership and management of land. In Leviticus, 25:8-13 states that prisoners should be set free, and people's debts wiped clean. It was a time of freedom and celebration when everyone received back their original property, and slaves were set free.

Lining
'Lining' was a feature of West Indian worship in the early years being in Britain. The custom was prevalent in America, especially the south and is thought to have begun in Gaelic communities in Scotland. Lining is when a designated person calls out the line of a song before it is sung with the singers responding by singing the line of the song. This process continues until the end of the song.

Mc Warren Walter Act 1952
The Mc Warren Walter Act also known as the 1952 Immigration and Nationality Act, limited the flow of West Indian farm workers to the USA. As a consequence, Jamaicans were particularly responsive to Britain's recruitment drive to work in Britain

Open Air Meeting/Service

These were church services which West Indians held on busy main streets or near to street markets both as a way of evangelising and also as a way of attracting people to their churches.

Pardner

A pardner is a rotating saving scheme in which family and friends save together which was once very popular in Caribbean communities, providing financial resources to buy homes, churches, significant purchase when most Caribbean people couldn't access resources from the financial institutions in the country.

Pastor

The name of a minister or clergy in a Pentecostal church.

Pentecostals

See Holiness Churches

Prayer Meetings

Church services usually held in people's homes during the early years of West Indian Christian's arrival in Britain.

Saints

A general term meaning members or congregation of a Pentecostal church.

Swinging Sixties

This was a period of social and cultural change in Britain. It's commonly known as the 'permissive age' mainly because young people who were at the forefront of this change took a relaxed attitude to sex and sexual behaviour. In music, The Beatles and the Mersey Sound were all the rage, and the pill, the miniskirt and the women liberation movement were all significant features of the time.

Spirituals

Formerly known as 'negro spiritual, the spirituals have their origins in the songs that slave sang on plantations as they worked. They are mainly Christian songs with themes from the Old Testament which slaves used to compare their position like that of the Children of Isreal who in bondage in Egypt longed to be free. Apart from having Christian messages many slave songs were coded messages on escape plans.

Underground Railroad

The Underground Railroad was a network of people and places that offered shelter to escaped slaves from the South. People who helped the slaves on their escape journey were known as "conductors." They provided hiding places in private homes, churches and schoolhouses. These were called "stations," or "safe houses," and "depots." The people operating them were called "stationmasters." Escaping slaves would walk at night for obvious reasons and when needed 'Wade in the Water' so that pursuing dogs could not smell their tracks. Spirituals such as, 'Wade in the Water, The Gospel Train, and 'Swing Low Sweet Chariot' directly refers to the Underground Railroad.

Printed in Great Britain
by Amazon

62923597R00099